OVERCOMING THE MOUNTAIN

A Manual for the Pre-Field Ministry of Deputation

By Nicholas Zarrella

Disclaimer

The author of this work has quoted the writers of many articles and books. This does not mean that the author endorses or recommends the works of others. If the author quotes someone, it does not mean that he agrees with all of the author's tenets, statements, concepts, or words, whether in the work quoted or any other work of the author. There has been no attempt to alter the meaning of the quotes; and therefore, some of the quotes are long in order to give the entire sense of the passage.

Address All Inquiries To:
THE OLD PATHS PUBLICATIONS, Inc.
142 Gold Flume Way
Cleveland, Georgia, U.S.A. 30528

Web: www.theoldpathspublications.com
E-mail: TOP@theoldpathspublications.com

Dedication

I dedicate this book to the Lord Jesus Who, by His grace, called me to the mission field of Japan and my wife, Lorena, for her strength and faith in endeavoring to care for our home and ministry.

Nicholas Zarrella, Master of Divinity
October 2021

Foreword

On more than one occasion, I, like you, have discovered the truth Solomon wrote about in Ecclesiastes 12 when he said, "Of making many books there is no end; and much study is a weariness of the flesh." Especially have I, like you, discovered this with books about ministry. Books that promise delight, but become a weariness because of a lack of depth, understanding, and practical application.

On other occasions, I have discovered the opposite side of the truth coin when Solomon wrote about acceptable or delightful words; words written with truth and application to bring blessing, direction and stability to one's life. These are the words that you will read in "Overcoming the Mountain: A Manual for the Pre-field Ministry of Deputation." Missionary Nick Zarrella has written a passionate, purposeful, and practical manual to help pastors, missionaries, and the church understand the ministry of Pre-field Deputation.

As I sit to write this foreword, our church has received multiple letters of resignation from missionaries that we support. Some have been on the field already and some on deputation. I cannot help but think if they could have read this book what a help it would have been to them. I once heard a pastor say, "Preparation is paramount to preventing the enemy." I believe "Overcoming the Mountain" is needed preparation for both the pastor and missionary. The practical teaching comes from a missionary's heart and experiences and flows easily into personal application that will help our missionaries overcome the mountain of deputation.

I know you will be blessed reading this book and I am excited to see how God will use it in the lives of those called to missions.

Pastor Thomas A. Hunter Jr.

Plantation Baptist Church

Table of Contents

Preface

When my family and I first commenced deputation, there was a shadowy image in my mind of the expectations of what was forthcoming. I had attended seminary, served in full-time ministry, and underwent missionary candidate school, but there remained a thick fog that surrounded the ministry. What was its overall purpose? How was it possible to raise the astronomical amount of financial support? Who was going to schedule with us to present our call? When would we finally arrive on the field? What were we expected to do when presenting in a church? Why did the Lord make it that we had to undergo this arduous climb? While our heart was in Japan, our bodies had to remain behind in America until we conquered this mountainous task called deputation.

It was during our travel that the Lord opened my eyes to the answering of these questions. Furthermore, through His wisdom I learned how to meet both the expectations of Scripture and of modern-day local churches unto the reaping of fruit for our ministry. While it is said that most missionaries receive partnerships with around 33% of the churches in which they present, we were seeing upwards of 75-80%. Even many pastors who welcomed us in with the caveat that they would not be able to partner with us, voted following the services to support our ministry. What was different? How were we receiving such gain?

It was through the observations of other missionary presentations wherein I noticed certain patterns, both positive and negative, that lead to either a profitable climb or an intense struggle on the rock face. It was then that the inspiration for writing this book was realized. While this writing is not guaranteeing the missionary an increased percentage of partnerships per visit (God alone brings the increase), the Lord had placed within me a desire to assist future missionaries in answering the shadowy questions of their heart, easing the burden of the ministry, and preparing them to better represent Christ and missions in the local churches of America unto the conquering of the mountain of deputation. I pray that this book has accomplished these purposes.

Introduction

Has one ever gazed before the face of a great and majestic mountain? It truly is magnificent to not only behold, but also to compare oneself to the sheer mass and magnitude of God's creation. What then if the task was not simply to gaze upon its being, but also to scale and overcome it? The process of deputation can be likened to the ascent and descent of such a great mountain. At the outset, standing at the mighty face of a behemoth task with the goal of conquering it seems impossible; as does raising the thousands of dollars of support required to reach the mission field. Even simply the visions of finally setting foot amongst the people of calling are eclipsed by the presence lying ahead. The purpose of this book is to give answer to the biblical and practical reasonings for deputation and to better prepare the missionary to efficiently and effectively "conquer" this mountainous ministry in the power of the Lord.

Missionary work is exhilarating and intimidating as one fantasizes about living and ministering amongst a foreign people. I have personally spoken to several individuals who have expressed a hunger and felt God's convicting call, but were nervous, or even turned away, at the thought of deputation. One can understandably sympathize. There has been very little accessible study or information disseminated for the regular church member. To the devil's delight, most of what has circulated are the horror stories that some missionaries have experienced while on the road. Certainly, horror stories do exist (some are unquestionably embellished), but they occur far less often than what is commonly perpetuated. Rather, I wish it were the many rich and wonderful blessings that would ring in the ears of God's people.

While moving forward in faith requires a complete trust in the Lord Who knows the "rockface," there is peace and comfort in gaining the general wisdom of the process as one prepares for the conquest ahead. Therefore, this manual will unpack that information by serving as a basic guide map for the ascent and descent of the mountain. While every missionary has commonalities and unique characteristics that are intricately woven by God, even these elements can be fine-tuned to fit the descriptions founded in this manual for one's personal life and deputation ministry. I pray the content is a blessing, an encouragement, a bolstering for the current state of missions, and an open door for those who are nervous, but yearning to surrender to God's calling on their lives.

Chapter 1
The Call to the Field

Bill McChesney was a missionary to the Congo. It was at 28 years of age that rebel forces had captured the malaria-weakened young man and proceeded to beat him to death. One of the lasting tributes of his life was a poem he wrote entitled "My Choice,"

> I want my breakfast served at "eight,"
> with ham and eggs upon the plate;
> A well-broiled steak I'll eat at "one;"
> and dine again when day is done.
> I want an ultramodern home,
> and in each room a telephone;
> Soft carpets, too, upon the floors,
> and pretty drapes to grace the doors.
> A cozy place of lovely things,
> like easy chairs and innersprings,
> And then I'll get a small TV –
> of course, "I'm careful what I see."
> I want my wardrobe, too, to be
> of neatest, finest quality.
> With latest style of suit and vest,
> why shouldn't Christians have the best?
> But then the Master I can hear,
> in no uncertain voice, so clear,

"I bid you come and follow Me,
the lonely Man of Galilee."
"Birds of the air have made their nest,
and foxes in their holes find rest;
But I can offer you no bed;
no place have I to lay My head."
In shame I hung my head and cried. How
 could I spurn the Crucified?
Could I forget the way He went,
the sleepless nights in prayer He spent?
For forty days without a bit,
alone He fasted day and night;
Despised, rejected – on he went,
and did not stop till veil He rent.
A man of sorrows and of grief,
no earthly friend to bring relief –
"Smitten of God," the prophet said –
Mocked, beaten, bruised, His blood ran red.
If He be God and died for me,
no sacrifice too great can be
For me, a mortal man, to make;
I'll do it all for Jesus' sake.
Yes, I will tread the path He trod.
No other way will please my God;
So, henceforth, this my choice shall be,
my choice for all eternity.

I believe the life of Bill McChesney and the content of
his words echo the very heart of those surrendered unto
Christ's call. Missionaries have labored in the jungles, in the

country-sides, in the cities. They have taught amongst the tribes, the civilized, the radical. They have endured persecutions, and hardships, and death. They have withstood the most fiery of darts for which the devil holds in his arsenal. Hands and feet have bled and lives have been lost. Most have never even seen the blessed end result of their earthy labors for Christ; having passed on before the bearing of fruit. All performed simply for the opportunity to heed the call of Christ in carrying His cross and His Word to the distant highways and byways of the lost and spiritually dead. The missionary is a living sacrifice, a servant to the King, a voice in the wilderness that the name of God might resound in the uttermost parts. What a mighty work it is! But where does it all begin? How do men like Bill McChesney set their vision upon the road of cross-cultural ministry?

The genesis of the work commences when the man of God dies to the self and lives unto the Lord. When an individual places the strivings of fleshly pursuit under submission to the Spirit of the Living God that one might live out His will in service to a people group; either domestic or foreign. As any Christ-abiding servant acknowledges, the Christian is not to defer to his own path, but is to set forth toward wheresoever and unto whosoever the Master commands. As I traveled throughout deputation, the following was often asked, "Why Japan?" It is a legitimate question; one which demands an answer that ought to meet the criteria for a God-called missionary. The following biblical principles will shed light on how to answer this question properly.

The Biblical Call of the Missionary

It is often stated that all Christians are missionaries, but this is simply not true; at least in the context of the specific biblical call. While all Christians are commanded to witness of the Lord Jesus, there are those specifically set apart and called by God to full-time missional labor. It is a similar thought process to evangelism or discipleship. While all Christians are called to evangelize, there are those specifically set apart and called by God to full-time evangelistic labor. While all Christians are to make disciples, there are those specifically set apart and called by God to Pastor a flock. I believe it is vitally important to comprehend this distinction between the general term and the specifically called because if the church is not careful, they will send those which are profoundly sincere, but not commissioned by God unto the peoples of the world based on the general principle that "we are all missionaries." Essentially, if all Christians are missionaries, then no one is a missionary. As the calling of an Evangelist and Pastor finds source in the Lord, full-time missional work must never simply be a good idea to fulfill based upon a general principle. It must be regarded as a specific calling of God placed upon certain of His servants to go and minister to the unreached people groups of the world.

The biblical accounts of surrendering to missionary work were not founded on an individual's personal impulses, of an honest and passionate sincerity, nor even of simply yearning to reach the lost. While some or all of these are secondary reasonings, they cannot be the mainstay. The predominant factor in the biblical prescription for entering full-time missionary service as displayed in the Bible was when the very Word of God was voiced unto those He had called to the labor fields and were then, in the New Testament, authorized by a local church to serve as their representative. It is a heavenly calling, a divine consigning, by the power and authority of the Lord Jesus Christ upon certain individuals to enter a spiritual work that is carried out beyond the walls of one's physical, local church body. Though the biblical missionaries were passionate and loving, it was not their emotions that were driving them, but the authority of the Lord and their sending church.

The Source of Calling is God

The Source of the missionary calling may be clarified through the words of my professor. He stated, "The predominant factor in being a missionary is not in the salvation of the heathen. If the reason you are going is for the heathen, then the reason you leave is because of the heathen. Isaiah said, 'Send me' Why? 'Because mine eyes hath seen the King, the Lord of hosts.'" His words have long had an impact on my heart. Why Japan? It is not because I find my strength and calling in the people of that nation. I love them and greatly desire for their eyes to turn unto the Lord, but the reason for my going is because Christ Jesus Himself had plucked me out of following my own will and called me to those fields of labor. Missionary attrition today is a real and increasing problem. It is certainly likely that a major reason for this is because many that are surrendering are doing so because of a burden for a people, but yet are not divinely appointed. A burden will only take a man so far past the starting line, but it has no power to sustain. The words of my professor find their source in the Bible and it is important to demonstrate from His Word that the call to the field must flow from the spring of Christ's will.

The Call of Ezekiel - Ezekiel 3

Ezekiel, a contemporary alongside of Daniel and Jeremiah, was called to preach to the Jewish people during the rise of the Babylonian Empire. During this time period, the nation of Babylon had twice invaded Judah, the Southern tribe of Israel, effectively taking many citizens captive. While Daniel and his companions were enslaved to serve in the Babylonian courts, Ezekiel was delivered to the refugee camps.

The purpose of Ezekiel's prophetic ministry was to proclaim of the coming fall of Jerusalem, the destruction of the Temple, the total annihilation of the city for the sin of the people, and then the hope and restoration to come in the future Kingdom of God. Ezekiel chapter 3 is the key focal point of this section because it emphasizes God's call for his prophet. In this chapter, the Lord fills Ezekiel with His Word (*Eat this roll*) and then commands him to preach that Word to His people in the refugee camps (*Son of man, go, get thee unto the house of Israel, and speak with my words unto them*). In the midst of his call, God informs him that the people will not only refuse to heed the Word, but will also make themselves harder than stone in rejection toward his ministry (*for they will not hearken...as an adamant harder than flint*). He is then carried by the spirit to the River of Chebar to observe the sin of the people he is to deliver God's Word, but the Bible declares he went *in bitterness* and *in the heat of my spirit*. There was an intense bitterness and rage that fumed internally within his spirit. I think it possible to sympathize with these strong emotions. It was painful to hear from God Himself that the people both he and the Lord loved, the people he was called to deliver the Word of God unto, would outright reject His message in venomous opposition. He was angry for their stiff-necked rejection, grieved for their blatant sin, and burdened for their refusal to hear from the Lord their God. Yet, even in this emotional state, the Bible ends verse 14 by declaring, *"but the hand of the Lord was strong upon me."*

This most important verse perfectly blends with my seminary professor's declaration. If Ezekiel's call was predominantly founded in his desire for the salvation of the Jewish heathen, he would have been consumed by his bitterness and rage. If the heathen were his reason for preaching, the heathen would have been his reason for leaving the ministry. He loved the people and desired for them to repent, but it could not have been solely his great love for them that strengthened him. As it was the Lord Who called him, it was the Lord Who sustained him. Ezekiel was fortified to press on not by the hand of men, but of God; likewise, must the contemporary missionary.

The Vision for the Gentiles - Acts 10-11:18

In the early development of New Testament missionary work, the Lord had called upon Peter to serve as His vessel for the receiving of Gentiles into the fold of Christ. Peter and the Jewish believers had not yet fully adopted the plan of God in the reception of non-Jews; hence, their strong contention in these chapters.

During a time of prayer, God placed him in a trance in which he witnessed a vessel descending upon the earth; wherein were all manner of animals, common and unclean. The Lord had commanded him to slay and eat, to which he refused on basis of keeping Mosaic Law. God had then informed him that He had cleansed these creatures, thus they were viable to consume. This vision occurred a total of three times, ensuring its divine establishment. While Peter pondered on its interpretation, a Gentile, Cornelius, approached him.

The account develops that Peter obeyed the Lord, the Gospel was preached, and the Gentiles received the Holy Spirit. The issue arrives in Acts 11 when word of his actions had reached the ears of certain Jews in Jerusalem. The Bible records that these contending Jews were *of the circumcision.* They still held tightly to the Mosaic Law, not yet fully comprehending that Christ had fulfilled it. Therefore, they contended with Peter in his eating and fellowshipping with uncircumcised Gentiles. Peter's response is absolutely vital for missionary calling because it highlights the divine reasoning for his work. The Scriptures record that he rehearsed what had transpired from the very beginning by expounding unto them the vision, the command, the three-fold nature of the trance, the Gentile men who approached him and their testimony, his giving of the Gospel, the filling of the Holy Ghost upon them, and the Word of God in Scripture as evidence for the Lord's will. The response? The Bible records, "*When they heard these things, they held their peace,*

20

and glorified God, saying, Then hath God also to the Gentiles granted repentance unto life." They could not war against the Word and will of the Lord. Though they were once in contention, they then were convicted of the truth and gave praise and glory unto Christ.

One may assume the difference in the response of these lawful Jews if Peter's reasoning was entirely encapsulated by emotional argumentation. It was the voice of God which had power to convict all parties involved. If the decision for the work was based on emotional discharge or personal conviction, the work would not have been accomplished. The Word has the power. It was actually anti-thesis in the mind and heart of Peter and the Jews to *"slay and eat,"* but they were given the Word. It was His calling and His will made known unto His choice servant. As Peter humbly declared, *"What was I, that I could withstand God?"*

The Separation at Antioch - Acts 13

Acts 13 opens by referencing a church, a leadership, and a ministry. The church at Antioch was raising leadership within its own ranks and, in the midst of ministry and prayerful fasting, the Spirit of the Living God entered into the picture to dictate His will for two of His choice servants: Paul and Barnabas.

Until this moment, these men were often serving the Lord. They loved God and they loved people. Barnabas was the *"son of consolation;"* that comforting, uplifting presence. Paul both exhibited and wrote of love often. It was through their profound love that the Lord built a burden in their heart to reach and disciple people. Yet, they had not utilized that great love as a means to "send themselves" as missionaries. They remained in service at their local church until the moment of separation in Acts 13.

As these two men had already established a notable history of servitude unto Christ, it came as no surprise to the church at Antioch when the Holy Ghost interjected Himself into their presence and stated, *"Separate me Barnabas and Saul for the work whereunto I have called them."* In the similar fashion that the Word of the Lord came to Ezekiel and Peter, it had likewise fallen upon these servants. Paul and Barnabas were called and separated by God unto the labor fields of missionary work.

The Macedonian Vision - Acts 16

Plotting forth in his missionary travels, Paul and his missionary band are soon met with a certain impasse of the Spirit for the next field of labor. In the beginning verses of Acts 16, they are seen as making disciples, preaching the Word, delivering decrees, and planting churches established in the faith. They were growing and increasing daily! Yet, when they push forward throughout Phrygia and the regions of Galatia, they are met with a halting to their steps. The Bible states that they were *"forbidden of the Holy Ghost to preach the word in Asia, After they were come to Mysia, they assayed to go into Bithynia: but the Spirit suffered them not."* With great momentum, why were they then temporarily withheld?

This act of God in forbidding Paul and his group to preach in certain regions was not that the Lord did not want laborers in those locales; rather, He simply had His specific will for this band of missionaries. They saw a great need for the lost in Asia and Bithynia, but that was not where the Lord desired to send them. Though they initially endeavored to enter those places, they obeyed the halting of the Spirit and stood by for His directives. It was in their waiting on the Lord that God delivered His will to Paul through a vision that directed their next undertakings in the region of Macedonia.

This account of Scripture contains an important principle of missions: It is not the missionary who determines the location, but the God Who called him. Paul assayed to enter into certain locales, but the Spirit forbade him. It is not that there was not a need or that Paul's heart was in the wrong. I believe he desperately yearned for the people of those regions to know Christ and to have churches planted amongst them. The problem that he found was that God determined him elsewhere.

I once heard a missionary family present their field of calling to a local church. God had called them to an eastern nation! With a heart of love for the people of that place, they declared the great need and their heartfelt desire to go and labor among them. When they relayed their testimony, they said that they had prayed, picked up a newspaper, saw a headline with the country's name, and commenced researching the nation and the need. It was soon following they claimed they felt God's peace and that His will for them was to minister there. When they formally presented, they waxed eloquently on God's peace for their life and their great burden for the lost souls of that country. It was only a few months following that they inevitably switched fields and commenced in calling their supporting churches and informing them that they never had peace for that eastern nation. Stories like this are common in many shapes and forms. An individual may be burdened on a missionary trip, or through cultural interest and fascination, or by a challenging voice in the pulpit to which they then determine that they no longer can stay on the home front. "How can I remain here knowing what I know? I have to go to fill the need!" "If no one else is going, I will!" "I have always loved 'such and such' a place!" While a burden for people is necessary, if God is not in agreement the endeavor is futile. Paul had a burden, but rather than trying to bend God and man to his will, he bent to God's. When man decides the work or the location, the ministry never flourishes. When it is of the Lord, the planted and watered seed is then given His increase.

God is the singular, dominating "Force" which determines whether one of His children is called into full-time missionary service. Whether in the Old or New Testament, it has always been God's voice in Scripture which declared unto His child His will for evangelistic, missional labor. Moses reasoned against Him at the burning bush, but he was called of God to enter again into Egypt and free His people. Jonah fled from His very presence, but the Lord sent a storm and a whale to deliver His Word to the Ninevites. John Mark had struggled initially with missionary work, but he was called of God to leave his home and thus was strengthened to labor in the fields. There are many men and women of God who have left the commonalities of their own lives to minister in lands and amongst peoples and tongues unknown; all for the sake of heeding God's call and reaching the people for which they were sent. As God alone is the Great Separator, not the church nor the man, it is His voice which determines the who and the where His servants will go.

The Sending Agency is the Local Church

William Carey had a dear friend and brother in Christ named Andrew Fuller. Preceding his departure for the mission field of India, Carey spoke this famous phrase, "I will go down into the pit, if you will hold the ropes." This dear friend did just that. He served as the President of the Baptist Mission Society and traveled around to various congregations preaching on missions and the great need to support the work. It was through his efforts that men like William Carey could serve in the "pits," while those that remained behind would "hold the ropes."

The medium for accomplishing God's work in this world is the local church. A missionary is never on an island of their own selves. As they minister on the field, the local churches they partner with are to secure them. As individuals are called by the Lord, it is His design that the local church would authorize and send. The following demonstrates this truth.

The Missionaries of Antioch

While the call of God on Paul and Barnabas was detailed above, the church at Antioch then had a duty to perform. The leadership moved swiftly when the Lord had made His will known. They set a date for an ordination service, prayed and fasted for the coming moment, and then laid their hands on these two missionaries (Acts 13:1-3). It is also highly likely they were ordained in front of the entire congregation, given that they had reported back to the whole church body during their furlough (Acts 14:27). This was the genesis of the missionary labors of Paul and Barnabas. The Holy Spirit then guided them to the "where." The many countries and cities and towns they would travel and preach the Word unto the salvation of souls and discipling of believers. God called, God commissioned, and God determined; it was upon the local church and the individual believers to heed His voice.

The Missionary of Jerusalem

Following the conclusion of the Jerusalem Council in Acts 15, Paul and Barnabas sought to return to the church in Antioch to relay the report of the conclusions of the assembly. Yet, it pleased the church of Jerusalem to send two men of good rapport alongside: Judas and Silas. These two individuals had a notable history of ministerial service and were recommended as godly representatives. Thus, they were sent alongside to tell the church family at Antioch *the same things by mouth* (the conclusions of the council). Following their report, the Bible records that Judas had returned to the church in Jerusalem, but Silas remained. It is at this pivotal point in Silas' life that he was called into the missionary fields of labor. The questions one must answer are whether or not he was called by God and if the church of Jerusalem authorized his sending.

In answering the calling of God, one must look to the Scriptures in 1 Thessalonians. While writing to the church, Paul introduces the letter by recording his name alongside Silas and Timothy. In chapter 2, he writes of their coming and sufferings and boldness in Christ. He then pens, *"But as we were allowed of God to be put in trust with the gospel."* That word *allowed* holds the idea of "examined, proven, put to the test."[1] Essentially, their past work in the ministry and dedication unto the Lord, as was written about Silas by the church in Jerusalem (Acts 15:25-27), had served as the proof of examination in Christ to be entrusted with the missionary work of the spreading of the Gospel. God had first proven Silas, and then, determined through His will alone, called this faithful servant to the missional fields of labor.

In answering if the church of Jerusalem commissioned him in recognition of God's call as a full-time missionary, the context of Acts 15 is crucial in displaying that Silas did abide in their authority. Though both he and Judas were sent to Antioch by letter and both were subsequently released to return to Jerusalem, it can be seen from Acts 15:40 that the leadership therein had agreed in the Lord to allow Silas to continue with Paul as a missionary, *"Paul chose Silas, and departed, being **recommended** by the brethren unto the grace of God."* (Emphasis mine)." That recommendation was an entrusting, a commending unto the grace, or the calling in this context, of God. They stood in agreement with the voice of the

---

[1] William Arndt et al., *A Greek-English Lexicon of the New Testament and Other Early Christian Literature* (Chicago: University of Chicago Press, 2000), Pg. 255.

Lord and the man of God for the work to be accomplished.

Silas was a man chosen by God and recommended by the church in Jerusalem to labor as a missionary. Did he love those he was called? Of course. In recognition of their love for the Thessalonians, Paul wrote, "*So being affectionately desirous of you, we were willing to have imparted unto you, not the gospel of God only, but also our own souls, because ye were dear unto us.*" They had a profound depth of love for people, but it was not predominantly their love or burden for people that drew them. Silas and Judas both *hazarded their lives for the name of our Lord Jesus Christ,* but only one was called and sent. Why? It is because God is the Appointer, the church is the medium that reckons and authorizes that appointing, and the missionary is the vessel which obeys and goes under the authority of both. God appoints, the church authorizes, and the missionary goes.

The Missionary of Lystra

When Paul arrived in Derbe and Lystra in Acts 16, he met Timothy; regarded as a disciple. Though he was but a youth, he was growing mightily in the Lord. As it was important to answer the questions of Silas' call and commissioning, the same must be accomplished with Timothy.

In answering his calling of God, one may simply include him in the verses written above in 1 Thessalonians 2. Timothy's name is recorded alongside Paul and Silas as one *allowed of God.* In granting unto him the same prescription afforded unto Silas, Timothy was clearly divinely appointed as a missionary. Furthermore, his later calling into pastoral service is evidenced in 1 Timothy 4:14 and 2 Timothy 1:6-9 will speak on his obedience to God. These verses indicate that Paul and the church laid hands on him in recognition that he was given *the gift of God…Who hath saved us, and called us with an holy calling, not according to our works, but according to his own purpose and grace, which was given in Christ Jesus before the world began.* As Timothy was subservient to the Lord and the church in his calling to pastoral ministry; likewise, was he in his years of mission's work. He and Paul and the churches understood that God does not call *according to our works, but according to his own purpose and grace.* Why was Silas called and Judas not when they both performed the works of the Lord? God's purpose and grace. Why was Timothy called to missional ministry and then to serve as the Pastor of the church of Ephesus? God's purpose and grace.

In answering if a local church commissioned Timothy in recognition of God's call as a full-time missionary, the Bible records that he was *well reported of by the brethren that were at Lystra and Iconium* (Acts 16:2). Who were these brethren? Were they simply those without a local church body? Absolutely not. In Acts 14, Paul and Barnabas had traveled to Lycaonia, wherein were the cities of Lystra and Derbe (and nearby Iconium), and they preached the Gospel. Though there was contention throughout these times of travel, the Bible records of the salvation of souls and the disciples made in these cities (14:20-22). This was the recordings of the early establishments of churches in these locales. When Paul returns to this area in Acts 16, it is clear that the churches he had planted had grown and were discipling believers of their own; including young

Timothy. When Scripture declares that Timothy was *well reported of*, it is simply noting that Paul and the churches had recognized the calling of God on this young man and had authorized his sending off unto missionary service.

Timothy was a man chosen by God and recommended by the brethren through the churches of these areas. When looking at his persona, he was somewhat sickly (1 Timothy 5:23) and may not have been the most courageous (2 Timothy 1:7, 1 Corinthians 16:10). The Apostle Paul would often write to him with militaristic language that he might fulfill the calling of God upon his life (1 Timothy 1:18, 5:21, 6:13, 2 Timothy 4:1). Regardless of his seeming personality, the Lord had His specific will for his life and the churches reckoned that calling. Again, God appointed, the church authorized, and the missionary went.

The same formula is continually founded in the Word of God: God appoints, the church authorizes, and the missionary goes. The missionary is not on an island of their own selves and the faithful men of Scripture continually set themselves under the authority of the Lord and the local church when undergoing missionary endeavors. This is vital to deputation because the missionary cannot simply bypass church agreement in their going and church support for their long-term plans of remaining. If the individual is to be authorized by churches to be their delegate representative in a certain location, they must then have the capability to effectively communicate that God has called them unto a certain field and, as Paul, Barnabas, Silas, Timothy, and many other missionary servants of the Lord were, be recommended by the brethren as one of good report.

The Modern-Day Call to Missions

It is vital to connect the narratives of the calling of biblical missions to the modern-day world. God has not changed, nor have His methods of raising up and calling out His people. By reading the testimonies of missionaries today, it will help to bridge the Biblical world with the contemporary missionary's own calling.

The Bailiwick of Guernsey

A missionary had presented at my home church for his calling unto his homeland. For his safety and anonymity, we will call this brother "Samuel." The entire congregation had never heard of this nation and were intrigued by his story. He was born in the Bailiwick of Guernsey, a tiny island near the coast of France. In 1981, he moved to California where he met his wife. During these years, he was a lost soul indulging in alcohol, selfishness, and materialism. His wife, a saved woman, had become involved in a program at their church; for which he participated to ensure she arrived home at a decent hour. It was during these moments of service that he was convicted and received Christ as his Savior.

After some time of growth, maturation, and serving in the faith, it was during their church mission's conference in 2015 that this couple had surrendered to full-time missions. For years they had been praying that the Lord Jesus would raise up a preacher of the Word in Guernsey, but that need had yet to be met. The difficulty was found in that, unless you were a resident of Guernsey, there was only a five-year work license available. Therefore, after five years any missionary preacher was forced to leave the country. Many churches were left without a pastor and had closed over the years. The law of Guernsey declared that an individual had to reside in that nation for twenty-three consecutive years to be "grandfathered" into the nation as a resident.

As he and his wife were praying for the Lord's ultimate destination for their own missional work, Christ had made His will known through His Word in Mark 5:19, "*Go home to thy friends, and tell them how great things the Lord hath done for thee, and hath had compassion on thee.*" Brother Samuel believed the law of Guernsey would affect him, preventing him from returning to the island as a resident. How was it possible for him to *go home*? Unbelievably, it was during a survey trip that he was able to review his residential history, which indicated he had lived there for twenty-three years and three months, consecutively. The Lord, through His providential power and written Word had answered their prayers to raise up a preacher in Guernsey. He was able to *"go home"* and tells his friends about the great things the Lord had done for him.

This testimony is important because it mirrors how the Lord called men in Scripture. An individual is saved and is discipled in the faith, he then commences serving Christ in whatsoever capacity he is able, at a certain time the convicting hand of Christ for a work is manifest, and, upon seeking His confirmation, the Lord speaks to validate His will. No, the Lord is not going to send visions nor place his children in a trance as He had in biblical times, but He does continue to clearly communicate to believers through the moving of His Spirit and His Word. "God, we are praying for a missionary to Guernsey!" To which He replied, "*Go home to thy friends, and tell them how great things the Lord hath done for thee, and hath had compassion on thee."*

My Call to Japan

I initially had trepidation in sharing my testimony in this book. My desire was to withhold mine own that I might share the powerful working of the Lord in the lives of others. Assuredly, there are many missionary testimonies to select from! Yet, I know and cherish how the Lord has called me to Japan and I pray it blesses the heart of the reader. I encompass my testimony in what I call the Three-Fold Chord. This chord was given unto me by the Lord that I might know His will for my life and for all decisions that I make by His leading.

(1) The first fold of the chord is the burden. While I was home from seminary for winter break, a missionary to Japan by the name of Lavern Rodgers presented in our church. He was eighty-nine years old and, by the time his ministry was complete, he had served seventy years on the field. During his presentation, he had demonstrated the mighty working of the Lord through his life in the winning of souls, the planting of churches, and the establishments of a seminary and camp ministry. At the end of his testimony, he removed his shoes and placed them atop the pulpit and declared these words, "It won't be long and these shoes will be empty. Does God have someone in your church to fill my shoes and take my place when He calls me home to glory?" When he came to our church, it was at that moment my heart was burdened for the Japanese. I launched myself into this bubble of educating myself on the nation and people of Japan. I wanted to absorb

all that I was able about Japanese culture, beliefs, and ministry needs. At that time, I learned that the Japanese were the most unreached people group in the world; and my heart was broken for them.

I once heard a missionary presenting his field. During the slideshow, he displayed a picture overlooking a city market with hundreds, if not thousands, of people about their business. The veteran missionary that was present during the time of the taking of that photo proclaimed, "If Christ were to come back in this moment, how much of this would change? Would anybody notice?" In this restricted access nation, only 0.2% claim any type of Christianity. I have chewed on that statement in regard to Japan. If Christ were to come back at this very moment, the United States would be shaken. Millions would disappear in the blink of an eye, but what about Japan? Would anyone even notice? With a population of 126,000,000 people and only 0.58% claiming any type of Evangelical Christianity (relative to the timing of this writing), would there be a trembling in the souls of the Japanese? The answer is no, sadly. I desperately want them and pray for them to know Christ. I want to see the fallow ground of Japan broken up and planted with the goodly seed of the Gospel of Christ. My heart is burdened for this people. I have a love for them that I cannot explain outside of Christ. It was from this first fold, this burden, that the Lord progressed me further toward His call.

(2) The second fold of the chord is the agreement. I could not contain this burden within my own self. I needed to seek the wisdom of my church family. I remember the moment I requested of my pastor that I might know his

thoughts. We were driving together to visit a church member in the hospital, when I, hesitantly and fearfully, asked, "Pastor, do you think I could be a missionary?" I further sought the wisdom of Godly men within my local church that they might provide direction. I wanted to be as the wise that *heakeneth unto counsel* (Proverbs 12:15, 19:20, 24:6). The consensus agreement was that if God was calling, they would lay hands on me and send me out as a missionary. The key word within was *"if."* If God was calling, I needed to go… and they would send me. It had not yet been confirmed, but the burden was growing and my church family was supportive if the Lord purposed it.

The local church is the authoritative body that God has set in place to further His program in the world. I will say it again, the Christian is not on an island of their own selves. As was evidenced above with the church in Antioch and several other biblical examples, God separates and the church sends. After receiving the second fold of agreement from my church family, it was then the Lord Who needed to make His will known.

(3) The third and final fold of the chord is the confirmation. Without this fold, I would not have surrendered to missionary work. Therefore, I sought the Lord in prayer. It was in the coming days, a resounding verse continued to echo in my mind, *"For I have much people in that city."* The Lord had placed Acts 18:10 into my thoughts to confirm His call. At the time of this writing, 91.7% of Japanese reside in urban areas; a number that is steadily increasing. Christ had made it abundantly clear that He was calling me to this nation of cities. As if that was not enough to satisfy me

(it was), I later found that a mission board affiliated with my own and based in Japan had a website which, on the home page, the President of the board referenced this exact verse as a clarion call for Japanese churches to fulfill the Great Commission. How wonderful is the Word of God as He uses it to call His children into the fields and cities of labor.

While there are certainly unique factors in the call of the Lord upon each missionary, far too often I have heard an individual present before a church body and reference their burden for a people and even the agreement from their sending church, but the actual confirmation of God is either absent or confused with their burden. If God is calling one of His children to His work, He will make it clear through His Word. If one has not received the confirmation, seek Him in prayer and He will direct one's paths. As these unique testimonies illustrate, the modern-day missionary's calling will always reflect how the Lord operates in Scripture - *"Now there were in **the church** that was at Antioch... As **they ministered** to the Lord, and fasted, **the Holy Ghost said, Separate Me...**"* (Acts 13:1-3 [emphasis mine]).

Summary Remarks

An arrow has no capabilities of its own. By itself, it is a useless tool. Only when it has surrendered to the power and will of the bowman can it take flight and strike its intended target. If the target is the field, the distance between is deputation, the arrow is the missionary, the bow is the church, and the bowman is God, it is rightly to suggest that one can never expect to travel the distance of deputation to reach the target without the Source of sending power, the Almighty Bowman, and His tool of sending, the local church. As Jesus Himself stated in Luke 10:2, *"Therefore said He unto them, The harvest truly is great, but the labourers are few: pray ye therefore the Lord of the harvest, that **He would send** forth labourers into his harvest."* (Emphasis mine) Paul reiterates this truth in 1 Timothy 1:12, *"And I thank Christ Jesus our Lord, who hath enabled me, for that he counted me faithful, putting me into the ministry."* God alone has the authority to take His arsenal of arrows and send them whithersoever He wills.

It was when Bill McChesney was met with the Master's voice that his choice had eternally altered from self to surrender. It was when Paul and Barnabas were separated by the Holy Spirit that they embarked across lands and seas. It was when brother Samuel and I received His will through His Word that we forfeited our own endeavors and ventured to foreign shores. There is never instability nor questioning one's calling when the voice of the Lord is what has made His will plain. If the would-be missionary's eyes have not yet *"seen the Lord,"* do not expect church ears to "hear His voice." Deputation ought never to commence until one's calling is secure. The missionary that knows he is called is then able to confidently and effectively vocalize it while presenting in the local church. This is how to overcome the distance. When a pastor and a church can undoubtedly receive the verifiable testimony of the presenting missionary, they can then trustingly take him on for support.

Why Japan? Why such and such a place? *"Mine eyes hath seen the Lord."* If one is able to state that confidently, God has then made it clear in one's calling to full-time missionary work and the local church will assuredly recognize that calling. What a blessed privilege to partake in! If the missionary reader is anything like me, the next question on one's heart must be "God has called me and the people must hear the Gospel. Why then do I have to go through years of deputation?"

Chapter 2
Why Deputation?

Standing at the face of the mighty mountain of deputation and even simply processing the requirement to overcome it is a monstrous task in itself. This often discourages many would-be missionaries from following the will and path of the Lord for their lives. If one does commence the ascension process, it can often feel as though all of the fury of the spiritual world lies in each attempt at progression. Gravity, falling stones from overhead, seemingly secure rock ledges loosing themselves, and pesky critters; the missionary might often echo the same sentiment as Jacob, "*...all these things are against me.*" Yet, let it be known that soon the muscles strengthen, the skin hardens, and perseverance heightens as one makes way for the summit. At this point, half of the journey has elapsed. While there still is yet the descent until completion, the beauty of the moment is that the vision of the heart is no longer blocked by the enormous presence of the mountain. The country of calling can now clearly be seen in the distance. Furthermore, certain elements that once hindered progression, such as gravity, often tend to be an asset during the descent. It is not necessarily easy climbing the rest of the way, but with the goal in sight and momentum increasing, the coming day of finally conquering the mountain of deputation will soon arrive.

I fully understand the plea of the missionary when facing this mountainous ministry. It was following my initial emotional high of answering the call to Japan that I was soon met with the realization of the monumental task that lay ahead. In my immaturity, I complainingly questioned the entire process, "People need the Lord in Japan right now. Why do I need to waste years traveling America and raising support?" My mind would flicker to the old account of Hudson Taylor as he was met with the formidable and convicting question from a Chinese native, "'How long have you had the Glad Tidings in your country?' 'Some hundreds of years,' was the reluctant reply. 'What! Hundreds of years? My father sought the Truth and died without finding it. Oh, why did you not come sooner?'"[2] Why could I not arrive sooner? How could I withhold my going when so many were already plunging into eternal damnation without opportunity to, at the very least, once hear of the only hope availed to mankind? The need is great; deputation seemed a trivial, overbearing, pointless timewaster. How wrong was I!

The Biblical Basis

I have both heard and read that missionaries ought to strive to finish deputation as swiftly as possible. The thinking is sometimes perpetuated that if deputation takes longer than two years, the missionary is simply lazy. If all that deputation is determined to be is a rushed "ministry" with the goal of

---

2. Taylor, Howard. *The Spiritual Secret of Hudson Taylor*. New Kensington, PA: Whitaker House, 2003.

"getting support and getting out," what then is the spiritual purpose? We may put our holy spin on it, but the thought process reveals the true intent. Why bother to climb a mountain when there are other ways of raising support or making money that are more efficient and less taxing? Unfortunately, many modern-day missionaries are trekking through "alternate" routes.

While I do not believe deputation ought to drag on, I do know that God has a work to accomplish through it and, if rushed or avoided, it will go unrecognized and unfinished. When it is properly attributed, deputation has three elements of fulfillment that are utilized by the Lord for His purposes. These three elements are the confirming of churches, the raising of support, and the preparation of the missionary. All three can be founded in Scripture and connected to the deputation ministry and beyond.

The First Element: Confirming Churches (Acts 15:36-41)

Following the incident of the split between Paul and Barnabas, Paul and Silas banded together and progressed forward in missionary endeavors. Before they set out to plant more churches on foreign fields and in various regions, they had a duty to visit established churches as they had in Antioch. The Bible records that they traveled *"through Syria and Cilicia, confirming the churches."* As these were already founded churches that Paul had a previous relationship with, these missionaries were then visiting them and relaying unto them the same message they had received from the Jerusalem

Council and had spoken to the church in Antioch (Acts 16:4). One may designate this as a furlough for Paul, but for Silas it can be regarded as a form of deputation work.

During their travels, one of their main purposes, if not the most crucial of all, was the process of *confirming* congregations. The word *confirming* is an integral piece of this study as it holds the idea of "strengthening." How was this accomplished? As the verses in Acts 15:36 and 16:4 denote, *"And after some days Paul said unto Barnabas, Let us return now and visit the brethren in every city wherein we proclaimed the word of the Lord, and see how they fare... And as they went on their way through the cities, they delivered them the decrees to keep which had been ordained of the apostles and elders that were at Jerusalem. So the churches were strengthened in the faith, and increased in number daily."* The confirming was intrinsically tied to the delivering of the Word of God. The strengthening of the believers was accomplished through the increase of their faith founded in the Lord and His Word. Paul often sought to accomplish this strengthening through his writings and/or visitations (Romans 1:11, 1 Thess. 3:13, 2 Cor. 1:15.) During his travels, it is evident that he taught Silas and others this important aspect of missional ministry.

If the modern-day missionary has found himself incapable of properly strengthening churches, it is not the fault of the Lord nor is it a lack of personal eloquence. While effective communication will have its major section in chapter 4, for now one must comprehend that eloquence is not synonymous with powerful communication or the ability to strengthen a church. While it certainly is an asset and public speaking ought to be refined by every missionary, it is not a requirement. If one is incapable of strengthening churches, it is because of a lack of knowledge in the Scriptures. Paul (not an eloquent man) and Silas (gifted as a prophet) were both utilized by the Lord Jesus to preach His Word unto the confirming of congregations. One must learn His Word and speak His Word in the power of God, which will then act as the greatest service a missionary can bestow during deputation. Furthermore, when this strengthening occurs, there is a much greater opportunity to receive financial support.

The Second Element: Raising Support (Philippians 4: 10ff)

Reaping financial partnerships is a major requirement for missionaries. The ultimate desire is to reach the field fully supported for personal living and ministry expense. While missions is not money, missions requires money that one may go and accomplish the task of reaching souls for Christ. The consistent flow of funding is not founded in the pockets of friends and family (though some may choose to bless in that way), but in the local church. As an encouragement to the missionary, do not lose heart when a church does not vote in favor of partnership. Even the Apostle Paul dealt with this reality.

When Paul was writing to the Philippian church, he penned, *"Now ye Philippians know also, that in the beginning of the gospel, when I departed from Macedonia, no church communicated with me as concerning giving and receiving, but ye only. For even in Thessalonica ye sent once and again unto my necessity"* (Philippians 4:15-16). Despite his travels and service unto several churches of

Macedonia, only one had partnered with him in the Gospel. Though deserving for his ministry unto them, only one church gave unto him a continual contribution of support. Again, while writing to the Corinthians he chided them for their lack of funding. In 2 Corinthians 11, he wrote that he preached to them freely, but to do that he had to rob other churches, taking wages of them in order to service the Corinthians (2 Cor. 11:7-9). Though he was blessed by their prayers for him (2 Cor. 1:11), they were not giving financially to meet his needs. In fact, one of those churches he was "robbing" was the church of Philippi. Why did he utilize the term "robbed?" Understand, as a missionary that had come and served them, he had the full right to receive support from their church. That was the expectation, but they refused to financially partner with him for his services. He had already visited them twice and was coming again for the third time. Paul was essentially stating, "I used the support money from other churches to serve you, free of charge. You should have been supporting me for this service, but you refuse to and so I am taking from them in your stead..." Why would he do such a thing? He writes later, "*Behold, the third time I am ready to come to you; and I will not be burdensome to you: for I seek not yours, but you: for the children ought not to lay up for the parents, but the parents for the children. And I will very gladly spend and be spent for you; though the more abundantly I love you, the less I be loved*" (2 Cor. 13:14-15). He did such a thing because he greatly loved them.

The expectation of Paul, as should be for every missionary called by God and sent by the local church, is to receive partnerships in churches they present. Yet, the investment does not always come. Continual monthly support is expected though not sought after as the main purpose for serving because missionaries love people and desire fruit unto their account (Philippians 4:10-19), regardless of the reception and support of any congregation. Ultimately, unto the church of Philippi, Paul was able to speak to them about the spiritual fruit abounding unto their account because of their *"once and again"* investment in him; a word not extended unto Corinth or the other churches in Macedonia. Wherever it arrives from, know that the Lord Jesus already has blessed partnerships and support readied for His servant. Trust in Him to provide.

The Third Element: The Preparation of the Missionary

As the individual is first called to climb the great mountain of deputation, one must comprehend that this process also serves to prepare for the many ranges to come. The mighty mountains far in the distance that require greater faith; therefore, the Lord readies His missionary through three areas of preparation: physical, spiritual, and anthropological. In the following sections of this chapter, I hope to unpack the practical, preparatory matters for which the Lord utilizes through deputation in refining His missionary for the work to come.

Physical Preparation

This aspect of deputation is how the Lord readies the body and mind for the physical tolls of the field. When I was in grade school, I had a great love for exercise and weightlifting (those days have long come and gone!) I recall

45

in my peak I was able to bench press over 100lbs of my own body weight. It was an incredible accomplishment as I had, for many years, worked on my physique three to five times a week. I was able to reminisce on the days of having the build of a stick figure to then enjoy the achievements of my steady progression. I could also chuckle at a time, early on in my weightlifting journey, when I believed curling a heavy dumbbell 100 times would grant me much more swiftly the massive biceps I desperately yearned. After I finished one set of 100 curls with my right arm, I was too fatigued to switch to the other and, upon waking the next morning, I found I had over-exerted my barely developed muscles. For one week I could not extend my right arm past ninety degrees. The ignorance of my immaturity coupled with the impatience for swift and profound results lead to a painful, disappointing conclusion.

The purpose of this analogy is to illustrate the similarities between the steady progression of body development in the weight room to that of the physical development of deputation travel. For one to commence deputation with the most substantial of schedules is like attempting to develop massive muscles instantaneously; it will only lead to physical exhaustion, intense burnout, heavy fatigue, incapacitation, and grave disappointment. If the missionary and/or his family are not accustomed to life on the road, it is necessary to slowly build up toward greater physical resistance.

The Apostle Paul's three missionary journeys may even attest to this process. Though he was already a seasoned traveler, even he did not at first set sail for Greece, Italy, and

Rome. In fact, his initial stop (and final as he retraced his steps back to Antioch) on his first journey was to Cyprus, the hometown of his missionary accomplice, Barnabas (Acts 4:36). It was after this initial excursion, wherein much of what he had experienced culturally was more "common" with his own background (of course, there were certain societal diversities and nuances), that his second and third missionary travels grew more distant, more lengthy, and more uncommon in his cultural witness. I am not at all dogmatic on comparing Paul's travel schedule with the development of the deputation process, but there are certainly principles one can obtain by studying it.

Even though America contains much that is common, there is rich diversity within her borders. The missionary will often find themselves traveling through or presenting in various contexts of cities, country-sides, deserts, beach towns, and mountain villages in churches of tens, hundreds, or even thousands strong; each having its own local and ecclesiastical flavor. A growing schedule stresses constant physical demands to present the call to raise support in a timely manner, ensuring weeks and months of separation from family, friends, and the commonalities of life. It is necessary to more deeply inspect these demands as they are essential for the extremity of change to come.

Physical Demands of Life on the Road

The physical pressures of deputation are taxing on the entirety of the body. Exhaustion often secures itself in various muscle groups, in the mind, and in the will. These take the shape of long hours of sitting and driving followed by intense mission conference schedules, late nights and early mornings, familial matters to manage, tending to the daily needs of cooking, cleaning, washing, and packing, and dealing with unforeseen, unplanned (sometimes extreme) circumstances and issues. Certain of these may appear to mimic the regular schedule of life, but they can quickly develop into unbridled frustrations that are greatly compacted during time on the road.

Allow me to elaborate with biblical examples of physical ailment. During the first missionary journey of Paul, he and his companions were faced with persecutions and accusations. While in the city of Lystra, certain Jews from Antioch and Iconium, having persuaded the citizens, stoned Paul and removed his body from the city believing him to have perished. What an introduction to missionary life! Though this is an extreme case of physical preparation, Paul elaborates in 2 Corinthians 11 on the many physical traumas that followed. He details his being beating with rods three times, his stoning, his shipwreck, the perils he faced, the weariness, his hungers and thirst, his cold and nakedness. The Lord Himself even allowed a "thorn" to remain in his flesh. Why? That he might learn to trust in the strength of God; made perfect in his own weakness. The Lord Jesus had steadily ramped up the physical toll on Paul's physical body, until he learned to be content in whatsoever state he found himself by finding his strength in Christ Jesus (Philippians 4:11-13).

"But Paul is a different caliber of man! Who can compare to him? His experiences were extreme!" He may have exhibited a high caliber of godliness, but it was partially developed by the Lord through his physical circumstances. Furthermore, there are few examples in the Bible that do not include God's child undergoing some sort of physical toll. Abraham fought in war and was constantly tested by either those in his family or those in the land. Joseph was sold as a slave by his brethren, separated from his household, falsely accused, and thrown in prison for years. Moses experienced battles with Pharaoh and enemies in the land. It was even during a war against the Amalekites that God had him hold his arms high in the air with a rod in his hands. As long as his hands were raised, Israel would prevail, but if his hands lowered, the Amalekites would prevail. Time would not be enough to speak of the physical challenges of Ruth in the fields, King David in the wilderness, the prophets and their trials, Stephen and his martyrdom... Jesus Himself. No, the Lord does not send every missionary through extreme physical challenges as He did with Paul, but never have I heard a life of obedience and service unto God that is free from physical tolls.

How then do we find encouragement when these physical engagements arise? Missionary, know that when Abraham was tested, the Bible called him a friend of God. When Joseph was sold, separated, falsely accused, and imprisoned, he continued to serve and honor the Lord. When the arms of Moses sank, his faithful friends stayed them. When Ruth was met with little hope of a prosperous future, Boaz redeemed her. When David fled, he wrote psalms and sang praises. When Stephen was martyred, he saw the heavens open as he witnessed His Savior at the right hand of

God. When Paul was stoned and dragged outside the gates, he arose and re-entered the city. All of these individuals allowed the Lord Jesus to utilize their circumstances for His glory as they continued to press toward the mark of the high calling of God. We must find, as the Apostle Paul, glory in our infirmities that the power of Christ may rest upon us (2 Corinthians 12:9).

Separation from Family and Friends

One of the physical tolls placed upon the missionary's mental faculties is found in the physical separation from family and friends. This *usually* finds its greatest burden in the heart and mind of the wife and children. However and upon whomever the burden lies, steps must be taken to ease and comfort the pains of distance.

An account from my wife's testimony will speak to the struggle of separation. She was raised in the nation of Venezuela when political persecution was beginning to develop. After her father was threatened at gunpoint, they received political asylum and moved to South Florida, where some of their extended family had previously migrated. As they had left their life in Venezuela behind, family then developed into a sturdier stronghold as they relied upon each other for assistance, love, and fellowship. Birthdays, social gatherings, personal experiences, and many of the factors of life were often attended and known by everyone. When we were engaged and the Lord placed His call in our lives for the mission field, the stronghold of family became a barrier to her surrender. Family was all she had ever known... how then could she leave to the opposite side of the world?

This reality brought about many difficult, tear-filled conversations. Instead of my acting in patient understanding, my own heart was torn by the thought, "She doesn't want to do this." I shamefully had accused her of this many times. Unfortunately, I did not shake that feeling soon enough. Even through her assurances and our marriage, my heart and mind continued to question her willingness to obey the call. Whenever the tears of struggling to leave her family behind leaked out, the accusation of my heart met my lips and her ears. I was certainly not making this difficult situation any more pleasant. I praise God for His mercy because, despite my early foolish actions and words, it was Him Who quieted her heart through His Word. In her weakness, she was made strong by the hand of God. Though it is never easy to separate from close family (and it should not be), the Lord Jesus does give grace, comfort, and peace.

It can be said though that not every missionary is close to their own kin. Some might even look forward to that day of long-distance separation! There is also often the other relationship of separation that reaps similar hardship: Friendships. These are usually among the brothers and sisters of one's own church family. Those the individual has known for years, has served alongside, and has shared in deep struggles and victories. I often think about an experience we personally had upon returning from our first venture on the deputation trail. We were on the road for about 1 1/2 months and were longing to be home. It was a strange feeling when, first walking into our home church, certain friends and families we had known and loved had either moved away or passed into eternity. This actually transpired each time we had left to present the ministry for an elongated period. It was even more odd when we were met by a new front door greeter on a Sunday morning. As we were entering the building, she jovially declared, "Welcome to *our* church!" I thought to myself, "I'm not a visitor, I've been a member here for 10 years. I'm a missionary sent from this church. This has long been my home!" I was not angry toward her; rather, it was the pain in my heart boiling internally. The moving on of familiar faces is a difficult reality of deputation and missionary work, but it was one we never believed would occur so rapidly. We thought it may happen after our first or even second term, but never during deputation! Our home church was feeling less like home as our dearly beloved brothers and sisters were moving on and new faces were moving in.

In hindsight, I do believe this to be of the gracious hand of God, at least for our life specifically as He prepared us for the foreign field. As certain connections at home waned, the ease to transition to the field steadied. Instead of allowing the clouds of relationships to remain looming overhead, the Lord lovingly and gently scattered them away. Not that they were forever lost, but that they no longer held sway over the heart. It was during this stage that my marriage strengthened as we drew near to each other and our faith in the Lord increased as we drew near unto Him. The following are steps to consider that the missionary can employ to better ease this transition of separation:

(1) A first step in helping to ensure a smoother transition is to start light and build heavier over time. The desire of the heart to arrive on the field as soon as possible

must find balance with the wisdom of steady progression and the purposes of God. Instead of commencing deputation with a fully loaded, several months long presentation schedule, pray for churches nearer to home or schedule a home-coming within two or three weeks. There will certainly be great encouragement in seeing loving, familiar faces.

(2) A second step for a smoother transition is to spend time with family and friends when there is opportunity. Traveling and presenting is exhausting work and often the stint at home is a period of rest and rejuvenation, but be wary of ignoring the relational needs of loved ones. Deputation does not last forever; therefore, it is especially vital to spend time while there is time to spend.

(3) A third step to ensure a smoother transition is to communicate often. "Out of sight, out of mind" is a real occurrence and skirting responsibilities in maintaining relationships becomes easier and easier as a busy schedule grows. Communicating often, however it is accomplished, will soften the blow and comfort the heart.

(4) A fourth step is to plan the final departure for the field following a major holiday. This is not always possible, but there is wisdom in spending one final Christmas or Easter or even birthday before leaving. This can greatly relieve the heart as my wife often expressed her desire for enjoying one final Christmas before arriving on the field; referencing the incredible difficulty of her first one away from their home in Venezuela.

(5) A fifth step is to acknowledge that missionary work is not the sacrifice of family and friends, but the desire to

increase His kingdom. Eternity with Christ we have with those we love who trust in Him, and greater yet when those we reach will also enter in. I echo Paul's sentiment in the final words to the Philippians of those he won for Christ, *"All the saints salute you, chiefly they that are of Caesar's household."* How wonderful it is to write home and tell of those who will join in glory.

Family and friends ought never to be abandoned or lost because of missionary work. When the Apostle Paul ended his letters, he would greet those near and dear to his heart and was especially burdened when, during the end of his life, only Luke remained alongside him. When Hudson Taylor was bombarded by the onslaught of the enemy, he wrote to his mother and said, "I need your prayers more than ever." Physical separation will come, but the missionary needs those back home more than ever; therefore, ensure that hearts remain knit together.

Separation from the Commonalities of Life

I love writing poetry. It is one of the joys of my life as the Lord places a thought or phrase upon my heart and I transcribe it in poetic form. As I was nearing the halfway point of my deputation ministry and the shores of Japan were steadily and swiftly approaching, this thought entered my mind, "What awaits me there?" It was from there I penned the following:

> What awaits me there,
> Past the bluest, crystal oceans
> and cotton-patched skies?

What awaits, where the foamy waves
Crest upon the shores?

Where unknowns are commonplace.
Yet not simply untracked paths
And crooked corners, no,
They are the lining on the streets?

And sight and speech and sound,
Yea, smell and touch,
Are alien to my senses?

And the constant twiddling,
And riddling and racking thoughts;
Those millions of questions;
presently unanswered?

What of the faces and places,
That are not mine faces and places,
Those I have long known;
When I tread the road and broke the bread,
Whom I've loved on that have loved me?

What awaits me there?
I know not.
Although, it matters not.
I will go. Gladly, I will go.
For I know that He Who goes before me,
Awaits me there.

I was raised in a fairly large suburb in South Florida. I

grew up near the beach in a melting pot of culture, food, leisure, and activities. Suffice it to say, it was quite a different atmosphere from when we were scheduled with a church in Oklahoma. What was common to me my whole life flew out of the window as we passed through small towns that appeared as though they were from old country western films. We have stayed in locations where the beauty of Fall and Spring were most vibrant, and others where gun shots were heard each night outside of our bedroom window. Culture shock strikes even in America.

As was written earlier in this chapter, deputation will demand the missionary travel to various cultural contexts in America. There will be churches with a membership that tend to embrace and nearly envelope the missionary and others that are reserved and timid to approach. Churches in small country towns are vastly different from those in bustling cities. All of these inner-country, societal experiences are to prepare the missionary for the drastic diversities abroad. Furthermore, these experiences both help to develop the general spirit of the missionary in dealing with change and also to adapt to various cultural contexts.

The thought of "what awaits me there?" does not necessarily find its only culmination on the foreign field. Especially early on, this question may often pass through the mind and heart of the missionary as one is preparing to travel to a meeting with questions such as, "What will the church be like? What about the town/city? What are they going to feed me? Where am I going to stay? Lord, what awaits me in such and such a state? Is it bugs? Or mold? Or danger? Will the church members care properly for my family? Can I trust my baby in the nursery? How will my pregnant wife cope in certain environments?" As my wife and I prepared for our first stint of deputation, we were lost in our expectations. We had asked veteran missionaries on their experiences and, though we were given words of peace, it was difficult to shake those age-old horror stories of opening the front door to a Prophet's Chamber and watching as the ground itself seemed to scurry away into the dark recesses of the home. The what-if questions can often drag on and drag down the spirit of an individual.

I hope to encourage the missionary here. My family and I were greatly blessed, loved on, and encouraged by nearly every church we attended. There are always the outliers, but even then the Lord utilized those negative experiences to teach us joy of spirit; despite our conditions. Suffice it to say in the goodness of Christ, when we were met with such a dramatically poor experience the following meeting would often provide some of the greatest blessings overflowing into our cup. Both the blessings and the challenges were an opportunity for the Lord to develop our spirit into one of complete trust in Him.

It is also important to understand that there must be a balance between long-suffering and boldness. For example, my wife and I have never spoken our opinions, unless specifically asked by the Pastor himself, on whether or not we believed our place of residence was "up-to-par," but we also ensured to protect our family. Here are some tips to keep in mind for the traveling missionary to protect their family from unnecessary troubles:

(1) Bring cleaning supplies. Sometimes a hotel or

Prophet's Chamber needs a little once-over. This will help to keep sickness at bay and cause comforts to rise.

(2) Be firm, yet tactful with your familial needs. If one is not comfortable with strangers kissing the baby or if one's wife is not secure enough to leave them in the nursery, politely, but firmly speak up. If the children have schoolwork, give them their needed time. If one's wife is sick and needs opportunity to rest and recover, inform the Pastor and encourage her to rest. If she is feeling unkempt, grant her the moments she needs to beautify herself without interruption. In essence, know one's family and tend to them properly.

(3) Enjoy the different landscapes and cultures. When traveling between churches, schedule time to visit famous landmarks, local restaurants, and exciting attractions. There is a surprising amount of enjoyable ventures one can take that are either low cost or no cost (or even high cost for special occasions). Help deputation itself to be a delightful experience of discovery and wonder!

(4) Adapt and appreciate the cultural differences. Every church family will cherish a missionary loving on them, learning about where they are from, and showing an excitement in their lifestyle. If they want to treat the missionary family to a local specialty, enjoy and acknowledge their loving hospitality. Fully digest the experiences of cultural minutia. One may not relish every experience or enjoy every meal, but the church will love the missionary for loving on them and embracing their culture.

(5) Stop asking the what-if questions. Even if the missionary's greatest fears are realized and the horror of the

home or the spirit of the church is overwhelmingly negative, arrive as a light for Christ. When Paul and Silas were thrown into the Philippian prison for casting out the evil spirit from the woman of divination, the Bible declares that they *"prayed, and sang praises unto God: and the prisoners heard them"* (Acts 16:25). Light drives out the darkness. Not only did the Lord free them from their bonds, but He utilized their situation and their praises to draw the prison guard and his entire family unto salvation.

What awaits at the next hotel or church or such and such a place? Whatever may lie ahead, know that the Lord is there. These inner-country experiences are preparation for the coming days when the heart asks, "What awaits when moving to the field? What happens when common occurrences, and appliances, and schedules of life drastically transform? How is one to handle strange sights and smells and sounds? What does one do when the family is sick, or is having difficulty reading the monthly bills in a foreign language, or unknowingly and mistakenly infuriates a local?" Everyone handles change differently. Some are able to embrace the ebb and flow of cultural difference; others struggle to endure. There is no profit to what-if questions, but there is great value in asking the Lord, "What can You teach me and how can You use me; even in a place such as this?"

While there are many similar deputation experiences that nearly all missionaries face, there is also the unique path for which the Lord has laid down for each individual in preparation for what is to come specifically for their life. What those that are called can know is that whatever is to come and however one's personality leans, the Lord Jesus is there.

Allow Him to have His way in the physical trials of deputation, that the dross be removed and the gold refined.

Spiritual Preparation

I watched a documentary of the world-renowned mountain climber, Tommy Caldwell. The main focus of the story was on his ambition to free climb the "Dawn Wall" of El Capitan, Yosemite's most formidable rock formation. This was previously thought an impossible, unclimbable 3000ft task. After escaping terrorist abduction and accidentally cutting off his index finger, Tommy's career was prematurely declared as finished due to the mental and physical trauma. A mountain climber's ability to climb was in his fingers, for which one of the most vital of his was now gone. At this juncture, he removed himself away from doubters and fixated on conquering his goal. Years were given over to mapping a path and training his body, his hands, and his remaining fingers to face the challenge. While the world scoffed at the possibility, he had faith not simply in his physical preparation, but in his internal will and determination. On December 17, 2014, he commenced his ascent and, 19 days later, his name was recorded in the history books.

The feat of free climbing the Dawn Wall was an unbelievable human achievement that the world believed, regardless of the physical specimen involved, unfeasible. Tommy believed; and it was this belief coupled with his physical training that reaped the results. The missionary is faced with greater tasks than scaling the Dawn Wall. Man's temporal achievements pale in comparison to those of eternal, spiritual nature. Conquering the mountain of deputation is merely one mighty rock face; there are a multitude waiting in the balance. Though physical preparation is necessary and needful, spiritual growth is imperative if one is to effectively serve their purpose on the field. A belief is required that is far more profound than Tommy's because the battle for the missionary is not against stones without a will or whim, but against the rulers of the darkness of the world intent on halting the Word and work of God. A faith is needed that is founded and securely fastened in the very God Who formed the mountains. Therefore, spiritual preparation is requisite as it serves to stretch one's faith beyond limits thought possible. Limits that must be surpassed if one is to maintain the greater faith for the greater mountains of the field to come.

Stretching Spiritually through Prayer

"Pray for me-pray for me! I greatly need your prayers. I do not want on the one hand to flee from danger, nor on the other to court troubles, or from lack of patience to hinder future usefulness. I do need more grace, more of the spirit of my Master, more entire resignation to the will of God, and greater boldness too."[3] This is one of the many pleas for prayer from one of the most profound missionary prayer warriors, Hudson Taylor.

Prayer is like the handle on a water spigot. There is plenty of water available to be had, but if the handle is tightly

---

3. Taylor, Howard. *Hudson Taylor in Early Years: The Growth of a Soul.* Place of Publication Not Identified: Hardpress Publishing, 2012.

sealed the water will not flow out. Such is a closed, tightly shut prayer life. The blessings of God are readily available, but prayer is how to turn the handle and reap from His eternal reservoir. The missionary who makes the loudest rumblings for the Lord in this world is the one who has gripped Christ's heart in the silence of a prayer closet. Do not reach the end of one's days (or ministry) wishing to have spent more time kneeling before the Lord. Develop a constant and consistent daily prayer life. One that is deeper than scheduled appointments. One that is of profound devotion when the Spirit beckons His child to the throne of God. There is no power, no wisdom, no fruit of one's own handiwork until the request is manifest before the Christ Who can do it all. To fail to rely on prayer as the most powerful, most useful, most effective weapon in the Christian's arsenal is to essentially elevate one's own power and abilities over that of God's. Without voicing it or maybe even, at least on the surface of our mind, thinking it, our actions display our beliefs. The Christian must never elevate ability, eloquence, productivity, connections, or even sheer willpower. The power of God is unmatched; and it is this power which can only be reaped through intimate, profound prayer.

I remember going through an elongated lull in scheduling churches. It was a distressing, infuriating time as I spent hours day after day for nearly two months sending emails and calling churches. It was rare to even hear the voice of a receptionist receiving my call. I was doing the work that I knew to do by remaining diligent and making connections to open doors, but there were no bites at the end of my line. Discouragement was mounting. One night in the late hours, I rose out of bed and sat on my living room couch. I was frustrated and the tears began to flow. I cried out to the Lord, "You called me to this. You are supposed to supply. I've done everything I can. Was I wrong in hearing Your call?" My Bible was on the table in front of me and I asked the Lord for a word of encouragement. I do not typically recommend the "pray and open to a random Bible page" approach, but that is what I did. I opened my Bible and it fell on John 1. My eyes instantly homed in on verse 50, *"Jesus answered and said unto him, Because I said unto thee, I saw thee under the fig tree, believest thou? thou shalt see greater things than these."* I took that word of encouragement as the Lord speaking to me and saying, "A vacant schedule is the limit of your faith? Behold, thou shalt see greater things than these." I then praised the Lord for His Word and then prayed something along these lines, "Lord, I have come up empty. I can't even get someone to answer my call. If you want me to do this, you need to provide. I am asking for one church to schedule with us each week. I trust and I praise You. In Your Name, Lord Jesus, I pray. Amen." It was not a profoundly spoken prayer, but the Lord heard my plea. In a variety of different ways and forms, God provided exactly one church on our schedule every single week for months on end. It was during these times I intimately understood and experienced the power of Christ Jesus.

If a missionary hopes to endure the trials of deputation and the mountains of struggle to come thereafter, one must remain vigilant in prayer. The Lord commands the glory. If He is not receiving it, He will not bless the work. Therefore, He allows His children to drain the limited supply from their own reservoirs in attempting to succeed without Him (an impossible venture) that they might learn to seek Him for all matters. The following are some areas of prayer to consider for the missionary:

(1) Pray for the spiritual and physical protections of the family. The devil is going to rage against the family in attempts of derailing the work. I have a missionary friend who shared this story about his daughter (Names are changed for protection), "Last night, I asked Chelsea to pack her suitcase for the weekend. She answered with a sigh and said 'again? When will we be done with traveling? I'm tired of packing?'" After he spoke with her and encouraged her in the Lord, he said, "She understands and is excited to go back to Brazil, but, as a missionary kid, she's tired of packing and just wanted a 'normal' weekend." This may appear as a light conversation with a teenage girl, but it is dangerous ground as the devil seeks to pry his fingers between family members and the Lord through discouragement. I am thankful for the godly spirit of this missionary couple in raising their children to love the Lord, but many have quit the work because they have lost their family. Grab ahold of the horns of the altar and lay one's household before the throne of God. One cannot fight off the fiery darts of the devil by fleshly strength or quick wit. He is able, allow Him to perform His work.

(2) Pray for the ministry of deputation. Deputation is a ministry, never fail to understand it in such respects. If it develops into a tiresome task or needless undertaking, the missionary will fail to reap the necessary results gleaned from it. Pray that the Lord Jesus would allow one's life and testimony to be utilized for His glory. One will have opportunities to preach to a variety of age groups, connect on

a personal level with church members, and issue challenges for missional work. The great delight is found when, either immediately or even years later, God utilized the man as His vessel to call a soul to salvation and/or the field. As my testimony indicated, He used Lavern Rodgers in my life. I hope to do the same. Pray also for partnerships to be made. The missionary is not traveling to tour the country; rather, to fulfill the work of God. Pray the Lord will use oneself and open doors of support that, in His time, one will finally step foot in the country of calling. Pray for His work of preparation to have full enablement in one's life. Ensure one receives every drop of what the Lord Jesus has to teach; it will be more than needful.

(3) Pray for encouragement. I have often thought of an excerpt from the great classic, *Frankenstein*. In the earlier chapters, it tells of a letter written by seafaring captain, Robert Walton, to his sister, Margaret. He penned the words, "My courage and my resolution is firm; but my hopes fluctuate, and my spirits are often depressed. I am about to proceed on a long and difficult voyage, the emergencies of which will demand all my fortitude. I am required not only to raise the spirits of others, but sometimes to sustain my own, when theirs are failing."[4] The long voyage of deputation will certainly test the courage and resolve of the missionary, but it will also test the spirit of the man and his family. Though unlike Robert Walton, the true captain of the ship is the Lord Jesus. Hope resides in His hands. He does not fluctuate nor

---

4. Shelley, Mary Wollstonecraft. *Frankenstein*. Oxford: Oxford University Press, 2008.

distress; rather; He is steady and upholds. While the seas of deputation may grow turbulent, know that it is the Lord Who is at the helm. Therefore, one may sweetly rest from all distress in Christ and Christ alone.

(4) Pray for the country of calling. The dearest way to affect the people to which one has been called is to pray for them, even before ever meeting them. I heard a missionary once state, "During deputation, I prayed the Lord to prepare the hearts of the people. When I arrived on the field, I prayed the Lord to send those whose hearts have been prepared." The missionary must pray that the Lord Jesus will send His Spirit before one's arrival to chisel away the hearts of stone that, when delivering His Word, they will receive Him. Pray the Lord sustains their lives and no disaster befalls them. Pray for ministry opportunities, for the missionaries that are currently on field, and for the national Christians to have boldness and strength in the Lord. This will knit hearts together as the Lord prepares the harvest fields.

(5) Pray for other missionaries. Missionaries need missionary prayer. Do not misunderstand, it is not that the prayers of church members and family are not sufficient; rather, there is the knowledge gained through walking the same path that allows the individual to pray for specific needs that are unknown to others. The struggles and demands and lessons of deputation allows a depth of prayer between missionaries that is needful to lay before the throne. Paul did not cease to pray for others, especially those in the same fold of work as himself; likewise, the missionary should pray for the missionary.

I would urge the missionary, open the spigot. Pray and

watch for the downpour of His blessed provisions. Why attempt to climb the mountain through one's own strength? Why undergo unnecessary, time-wasting hardships? The Lord is readied and waiting to answer our prayer. Seek His face, He will assuredly make the way.

Stretching Spiritually in the Word

When I was called into full-time ministry, I believed my pastor would simply hire me, set me in some area of full-time service, and send me out. How foolish! I scheduled a meeting to share with him God's calling and moving in my life and the Holy Spirit impressed upon me within my own spirit to abide by the instructions I was to receive. After informing him of the call, he very calmly stated, "Ok, well... you're going to have to go to school." My heart sank! I already had a business degree and I was taking Bible classes online. I had just purchased a home and had responsibilities. There was no way I could just pack my belongings and leave to attend seminary! Yet, how could I argue with the Holy Spirit? It was God Who called me, His Spirit Who instructed me to listen, and His will for me to educate myself in His Word. I applied to seminary, packed my bags, and left to receive my education.

Educating oneself before, during, and proceeding deputation is necessary work. In fact, it ought to encompass a lifetime. The Apostle Paul testifies of this truth. After he received the Gospel but before his full-time missionary work, he was separated by God that He might *reveal His Son in me, that I might preach Him among the heathen*" (Galatians 1:15-16).

During this time, he was distanced from *flesh and blood*, a reference to other Christians, and it appears implied that he sought the Scriptures as the Lord Himself instructed him (Galatians 1:11-12). What is crucial to note is that it was God Who required even of Paul, the educated, knowledgeable Apostle, to learn the Scriptures that he might preach as a missionary amongst the heathen; a reality which would not fully take place for about another fourteen years (Galatians 2:1; Acts 11:25-26). Furthermore, his love of learning and growing in the Word of God encompassed the entirety of his life. As his days on earth were nearing the end, he wrote to Timothy in prison and requested of him to bring a cloak, the books, and especially the parchments. The books and parchments that he so desperately desired were the scrolls of Holy Scripture. Paul was a student of the Word and, through his studies, he was stretched by God to even greater heights of faith. Heights that sustained him, even during his years of trial, hardship, and eventual martyrdom.

Paul required a spiritually stretching of the Word. Timothy required a spiritual stretching of the Word (2 Timothy 4:2). Apollos required spiritual stretching of the Word (Acts 18:24-26). The missionary requires a spiritual stretching of the Word. It is the Word hidden in the heart that sustains the servant, gives power to the ministry, and builds up the next generation of leadership. When preaching and teaching, whether at home or abroad, the missionary is expected to have a certain depth of knowledge in the Scriptures. While many will not have the capacity of a Paul (a reality which ought to further convince the individual of their educational duties), the leaders of God's program are required to be trained in the Word that they might lead His church, disciple believers, and rebuke the wicked (1 Timothy 3:6, 2 Timothy 2:15, Titus 1:9).

One of the difficult decisions in preparing for full-time ministry is to suspend it in the present that it might have fullness in the future. Postponing the opportunity to plunge ahead into the field work for the sake of receiving a biblical education in a formal system is, in my belief, a prerequisite to missionary work. Note, it is a precondition to full-time missionary service, not part-time ministries or internship opportunities. Please understand, suspending the mission is not forsaking the mission. Preparing for war is necessary for success in battle. In his famous work, *The Art of War*, Sun Tzu writes, "The art of war teaches us to rely not on the likelihood of the enemy is not coming, but on our own readiness to receive him; not on the chance of his not attacking, but rather on the fact that we have made our position unassailable."[5] The battlefield of spiritual warfare is no place for the unskilled novice to immediately take the position of a commanding general. Preparation for war starts with basic training; readying oneself to withstand the attacks of the enemy. If the missionary is to make their position "unassailable," it commences in the basic training of the classroom. He must be stretched past his current boundaries of faith and knowledge that, when the enemy approaches, he has trained himself and the soldiers of Christ under his command to skillfully wield the sword of the Lord.

---

5. Tzu, Sun. *The Art of War*. Simon & Brown, 2010.

If God has called a man to full-time missionary work, He has also called him to receive a formal, biblical education before arriving on the field; whether that is through in-depth discipleship and teaching of one's local church or in a formal seminary environment. The fruit of this basic training is to make one's spiritual position unassailable. Reap everything available in these studies; it will find its blessed culmination on the battlefield of spiritual warfare.

Stretching Spiritually by Experience

William Ward, one of the contemporaries of William Carey, once stated, "We are only scholars. It rests with the Great Teacher to decide which lesson shall come next - a hard one or an easy one."[6] The lessons he is referencing are those of experience. Possibly, a missionary is a well-learned bible scholar and formal education has been the mark of his life; comprehend that there is still much to learn. Experiential training is as important in the preparation of the missionary for the field as is formal education. Book knowledge is limited without practical experience; and vice versa. The two are coupled by the Lord to refine His workman for his trade.

I believe one of the main goals in experiential training is to toughen the skin and soften the heart. The Apostle Paul dealt with this training often with the Corinthian Church. Their blatant sin, disregard for his authority, and failure to support him financially as a missionary caused him great

---

6. Carey, S. Pearce, and Peter Masters. *William Carey*. London: Wakeman Trust, 1993.

anguish of heart. Even still, he loved them, despite their lack of love toward him (2 Corinthians 12:15). He had tough skin. He was able to take both the whippings of the enemy and the knives of the brethren. It was that tough skin that helped him to endure mistreatment, but it was his soft heart that made his ministry blossom in the power of God. His living was sourced from the abundant love in his heart for the Lord Jesus and the people for whom He died. Unfortunately, the experiential training of the Lord has often garnered the polar opposite results for which He desires. Far too often, the skin softens and the heart hardens, until the man of God is old, crabby, and discontent. The voice of Jacob a constant, reverberating echo, *"All these things are against me!"*

This particular training is one the most difficult of all because it tries the emotions. A pastor once stated in reference to worship music that the rhythm of worship ought to be steady and orderly. He illustrated this by referencing the reaction of water in concert with music. When the beat is balanced and systematic, the water has a consistent, rhythmic pattern, but when the beat is chaotic and disorderly, the water is incapable of maintaining a proper shape and flow. This is often the case with emotion. When the ministry is steady and orderly, the flow of the emotions remains in line with the rhythm, but when chaos and disorder erupt, the emotions have a tendency to lose their stability. The important difference for which must be accounted is that water has no will, unlike that of the person. Emotion and circumstances must always be subservient to the Spirit. Paul was not a man typically driven by emotion, but there was a time when the rhythm of the moment developed into strong contention that he was given over to that state of disorder. It was at this time he and Barnabas split over the issue of John Mark (Acts 15:36-39). Suffice it to say, he learned from this emotional blunder as, later in his ministry, he desired of the profitable young man to join him again (2 Timothy 4:11).

Developing the toughness of the skin and the softness of the heart requires the Lord to act as the skilled carpenter. The skillset of a carpenter is to go about his trade of carving pieces of wood to fit a specific image. He will take his tools and shave off the unwanted parts. He will trim and manipulate in all of his skillful ways; molding and shaping the wood to fit his specifications. Eventually the image in his mind proceeds to take shape; the final product coming around as there is more trimming and shaping and intricate detailing to perform. Finally, after much time passes the product is complete and the image for which the carpenter set out to form is realized. His skillful work had transformed a slab of wood into a beautiful work of art reflecting the carpenter's very heart. Likewise, the missionary must allow himself to be a slab of wood in the Carpenter's hands. Experiencing the tools for trimming and shaping and manipulation hurts, but it is necessary work that one might reflect the image set forth in the heart of Christ.

There are those that have attempted to free-climb the Dawn Wall, fully believing in themselves, but have nevertheless failed to accomplish their task. Like a rubber band reaching its limit, human capabilities can only be stretched so far until they snap. The spirit within God's children has no such limit. There is no final capacity until the "snapping point." The reason is not because the individual is capable in himself; rather, it is because the Lord is the source of this unbreakable band of faith. I once heard it said, "I can't, but God can, so I can." This is the purpose of the spiritual stretch, of the trimming and shaping of the wood, of the flexing of the spirit. The missionary cannot accomplish anything by himself, but as his faith in the God Who can increases, impossibilities became the steppingstones to conquering the greater mountains ahead. As Hudson Taylor once said, "Impossible, difficult, done."

Anthropological Preparation

Mitsuo Fuchida was the Japanese lead pilot of the squadron that attacked Pearl Harbor. Following the war, he came to know the Lord and serve Him as an Evangelist. It was during this time that he encountered a Christian missionary league aimed at reaching the Japanese for Christ. The following was his assessment of their work, "Reluctantly Fuchida concluded that the league had failed in Kyoto and would continue to fail because it was attempting to convert people whom it made no effort to understand."[7]

Deputation grants years of critical opportunity to garner a vast amount of first and second-hand cultural information for the field of calling. This knowledge is a vital aspect of the success of any missionary endeavor because, as Mr. Fuchida declared, it helps the missionary to understand the people, which opens wider the doors for conversion.

---

7. Prange, Gordon William., Katherine V. Dillon, and Donald M. Goldstein. *Gods Samurai: Lead at Pearl Harbor.* Dulles, VA: Brasseys, 2004.

Rather than arriving on the field immediately after one is called and mistakenly committing an immense number of cultural faux pas, deputation forces an interval period between which, if time was well spent in anthropological study, helps to drastically limit one's mistakes. It also endears the heart of the people to the foreigner who has, in respect to their culture and custom, become as they are in all aspects not sinful.

Hudson Taylor eloquently presented this mindset,

But I have never heard of any one, after a bonafide attempt to become Chinese to the Chinese that he might gain the Chinese, who either regretted the course taken or wished to abandon it... It is not the denationalization but the Christianization of this people that we seek. We wish to see Chinese Christians raised up-men and women truly Christian, but withal truly Chinese in every right sense of the word. We wish to see churches of such believers presided over by pastors and officers of their fathers, in their own tongue, and in edifices of a thoroughly native style of architecture. 'It is enough that the disciple be as His Master.' If we really wish to see the Chinese such as we have described, let us as far as possible set before them a true example. Let us in everything not sinful become Chinese, that way we may by all means 'save some.' Let us adopt their dress, acquire their language, seek to conform to their habits and approximate to their diet as far as health and constitution will allow. Let us live in their houses, making no unnecessary alteration in external form, and only so far modifying their internal arrangements as health and efficiency for work absolutely require.[8]

8. Taylor, Howard. *Hudson Taylor and the China Inland Mission: The*

In all things, excluding the sinful, become as the people one is to minister. It is better to strive to arrive on the field as an African, or a Chinese, or a Guatemalan, or a Russian, or as such and such a tribe and people group; than to take one's first steps on foreign soil with the "American card" in hand that states in the fine print, "Forgive me, but my culture is better than yours. Now listen to the Gospel of God's love." Unfortunately, the American card does not often work on foreign soil; rather, it tends to leave a foul taste in the mouths of the people. The following observations are ways in which the missionary can prepare anthropologically for the field.

Survey Trips

Personal expectations very rarely reflect reality. Before visiting a foreign field, the missionary will maintain certain visions of the architecture, the landscape, the people, the culture, and the ministry that may or may not necessarily be true. I have a close missionary friend, let's call him Grant, that serves in Egypt. Upon listening to his description of the people, he emphasized that the Muslim world was not dominated by American hating, Christian loathing terrorists. Truth be told, most people groups already know the American's preconceived notions about them. He shared a story of a time, early in his missionary life, when he boarded an elevator in Egypt already occupied by a Muslim man and his wife. While the woman was completely covered in all of the trappings of Muslim garb, her husband caught Grant's

---

Growth of a Work of God. Nabu Press, 2010.

75

eye. With a sly smirk, he stealthily pointed to his wife and, with an obviously feigned seriousness painted on his face, mouthed the word, "Terrorist." This light-hearted story served to display that, while there is obvious danger serving the Lord in Egypt (and many other countries), stereotypes seldom match reality. Grant found the majority of people in Egypt to be hospitable, loving, and friendly, in contradiction to the typical American labeling.

The American view of various cultural groups is often shaped by the media and other sources. Stories like the above often shatter our own preconceived notions and force us to evaluate what a place and a people are really like. One of the best approaches to fulfilling that is to personally visit the country. The Prophet Jeremiah touched on this principle when he woefully penned the words, *"Mine eye affecteth mine heart."* (Lamentations 3:51) As he witnessed first-hand the destruction, the poverty, and the vile acts of desperate Israelites, his heart was deeply affected. His eye, not merely his ears, affected his heart. Reaping the opportunity to witness first-hand the great need of lost souls in another part of the world, entrapped by their own sin, often greatly affects and endears the heart of the missionary. It lights a blazing fire within the soul to climb the mountain of deputation and reach the great harvest fields of the country of calling.

Language Studies

I have often heard the advice given that it is better to forgo attempting to learn the language of the people while on deputation. The only argument I have heard (there may be others) to accepting this advice is because the missionary does not want to accidentally learn incorrectly, which would then create a situation where they are forced to forget everything previously taught and then relearn everything anew. While this may have held some standing in former years, it no longer has much credibility.

The world today is more connected than it ever has been through technology. There are numerous, world-renowned language learning apps, reliable study materials, and online classes from native speakers available at our fingertips. Unless the missionary is called to a little-known tribe with no documented language, it is preposterous to refuse to at least learn the rudimentary elements of the foreign tongue for which one is called before arriving on the field. While on deputation, I spent hours every day learning Japanese Kanji and studying grammar through top-rated phone applications that actually pronounced the words through a native speaker. If not for having to complete my seminary studies, I would have also taken an hour each week to sit with a personal, online foreign tutor and trained my ear to hear and my mouth to speak the words. My desire was to at least know the basics that I was not "fresh off the plane" when I arrived on the field.

Furthermore, language is rich with cultural context and cues that assist in the missionary's understanding. Catch phrases, greetings, endearments, and the like hold great sway in connecting with people. When one knows the heart of their language, one can speak to their heart. When one can speak to their heart, one can reach them for Christ. My wife often speaks of a certain missionary that came to Venezuela and served amongst them. What captivated her family and those in the city was that he learned the heart of their language. He spoke as they spoke, as if he was born and raised amongst them. It is at this level every missionary ought to strive.

Language learning, even for predominantly English-speaking countries, is a critical element to the success of every missionary. There is plenty of time available and many accessible, highly rated resources to utilize to plunge ahead of the learning curve. The anthropologic implications of studying the language pre-field are too weighty to refuse.

Cultural Studies

As with language studies, there are also plenty of cultural learning resources accessible for the missionary. These resources are both beneficial and dangerous because of their range of accuracy. YouTube videos highlighting cultural elements, religious celebrations, rules and etiquette, faux pas, etc. are readily available and often created by native people. I have watched a particular Japanese gentleman who records his own videos explaining various aspects of Japanese culture, but he always commences his uploads with this reference, "The content of my videos are based on personal studies and experience. There is no intention of denying other theories and cultural aspects." Herein lies the rub: Any individual can say whatever they want, it does not necessarily make it true. My caution for utilizing any resource to perform cultural studies is to confirm it in other locations before accepting it as fact. YouTube and other media can be wonderful tools to study a culture, but the content must be received with caution.

Books and documentaries are also vital tools for study. Learning of the religion(s) and history of the country will often paint the picture as to why the people maintain their current worldview. There are often former missionaries that have documented their work amongst the peoples and anthropologists who have examined the culture. Utilizing these studies and experiences, even if some past truths are no longer a part of the culture today, will greatly assist in the understanding of the people. Why they perform certain actions. Where their beliefs originate. What they aim to achieve in life and beyond. There are a multitude of questions for which the missionary ought to have learned and thought through before landfall so as not to be blindsided when confronted on the field.

Missionary and National Connections

A final piece of anthropologic study will come through the personal connections made with veteran missionaries and nationals. Having the opportunity to ask questions of those on the field and those that were raised in the culture is an invaluable resource. These are individuals that, if available, the missionary must glean from that they might be more effective in ministry.

Far too often, the coming generation lauds their newfound "wisdom" over older servants or native residents. It is foolish ignorance to reject the knowledge of those who have long labored in the fields of harvest. Glean from their experiences and soak up their wisdom. They have made mistakes and reaped successes. They have labored in the hard soil, tilling it for years that the seed might be planted and bear abundant fruit. Not everything is required to be accepted as true or right, but how sad for any missionary to arrive on the field only to trample the seed and soil underfoot because they refused the insight of an elder. These important connections will help to prepare, develop, and sustain the missionary moving forward.

If the missionary fails or neglects to understand the people for which they are trying to reach, they will have little success in the ministry. The heart of missions is to raise up disciples in their own culture that the Light of God's Word would shine forth as beacons from amidst their own people. Take up their dress, eat their food. In all things not sinful, become as they are.

Summary Remarks

The mountain of deputation is arduous, but there are rich lessons on each rock ledge. This ministry will try the heart, the spirit, and the mind, but they work together to strengthen churches and refine the missionary to be profitable unto the Lord. With the many great mountains set in the distance, the individual must not set his heart in attempts to bypass the perfecting process of the Lord. Remain patient, remain steadfast, remain joyful in Christ; this monstrous mountain will be conquered in His power and in His perfect timing.

Chapter 3
Building a Presentation Schedule

A concept from the life of William Carey touched on the important comparison of ploughing a field in relation to the ministry work: "The rule for straight ploughing: the eyes must be set upon a definite mark."[9] Building a presentation schedule can be likened to the task of straight ploughing. As the plow is the device required to break open the ground for planting seed and reaping a harvest, the current field of missionary labor consists of the monotonous task of utilizing devices to "break open" church doors to "plant" the seed of calling that support may be raised. The definitive mark in the distance is the place of God's calling. As long as the missionary sets his eyes upon that mark, the tedious work in the fields will have a maintained focus with productive, efficient results.

Plowing through church soils to build a presentation schedule is one of the more challenging works. The lengthy hours of attempting to open a line of communication and often receiving limited to nil response can feel as the most

---

9. Carey, S. Pearce, and Peter Masters. *William Carey*. London: Wakeman Trust, 1993.

unrewarding of the entire deputation endeavor. The missionary can fall into the pits of questioning the process, painting the churches of America with black, heartless stains, and/or bypass reaching 100% of their goal and arrive on the field under-supported. These results occur because the eyes have been taken off the goal and placed onto the current situation. God's laborer has focused on a plot of rocky soil that does not seem to budge under the force of the plow.

It was the Lord Who proclaimed, *"No man, having put his hand to the plough, and looking back, is fit for the kingdom of God."* (Luke 9:62) I do not mean to quote that verse as a discouragement to the missionary struggling with the groundwork. On the contrary, know that when one is tilling the ground with the plow of God, one labors with the God Who has all power (Matthew 28:18-20). Building a presentation schedule is strenuous work, but it is a major component of deputation for fulfilling the call of the Lord on one's life. The blessing found therein is that the missionary, rather than retreating back or stagnating, can progress forward with full confidence that the God of the plow is also the God of the soil. It is He Who will break through the hard ground and advance His plowman, laboring in the wisdom and power of the Lord, ever nearer to the mark in the distance.

The Representative Mouthpiece

A veteran missionary to the Philippines was on furlough and had come to report on the Lord's handiwork. It was during the preaching hour that he spoke the following powerful statement, "I am the mouthpiece for [*this supporting church*] in the Philippines." (Italics mine) I thought to myself on the truth of those words. As our supported missionary, he had been commissioned to preach the Word of God amongst the peoples of that nation for which we had partnered with him. As we could not go ourselves physically, he was sent as our representative mouthpiece because there was agreement between us in faith and practice.

Building a presentation schedule commences with knowing one's own faith, style, intentions, and convictions as partnering churches will hold certain immediate and future expectations. This is not to place the Lord's commands of holiness of self and ministry to the back burner; rather, it is wisely operating within His practical spectrum. Certain churches may or may not require of their visiting and supported missionaries' certain principles of music, dress and appearance standards, and other ranging areas of personal conviction. If the missionary is to "be their mouthpiece," it is only fitting that he represents amongst the native peoples in a way that is both honorable unto the Lord and is as likeminded in spirit as possible on the foreign field with one's supporting churches.[10]

---

10. This is not advocating for planting American-styled churches on foreign soils. This is merely understanding certain standards of supporting churches and honoring those standards. The chameleon approach of promoting oneself to a church as likeminded, yet internally maintaining the intent to labor on the field with drastically different "colors" is dishonest and disingenuous. Furthermore, everyone's true colors are always manifest at some point; therefore, the chameleon approach of raising support is rarely long-lasting or profitable.

Finding likeminded churches is not often a simple task. The *independent* in Independent, Fundamental Baptist is profoundly visible when the missionary blazes the deputation trail. Every church, every pastor, every building, every congregation, and every practice has the uniqueness of a fingerprint. While the fingerprint is recognizable for what it is, there are also three main styles, arches, loops, and whorls (all with certain sub-categories of identification), with each one independently unique. Such is the local church. Some missionaries may prefer a church that resembles arches, others may prefer loops, and certain even the whorls. While all maintain God's identifying mark, they operate with a slightly different bend and twist than another. The important part to remember is to maneuver as often as possible within one's identifying mark. This helps to ensure unity in person, in spirit, and in representation on the field as the mouthpiece.

This can be accomplished through various means, but I would urge the missionary to join a like-minded mission board (if a formal mission board is the route one has chosen) and/or a fellowship of pastors and churches with a similar mindset, vision, and goals. My family and I joined both a missionary service agency and a growing Baptist Church network that endorsed us as missionaries, effectively opening the doors for support from within their circles and ensuring a continual fellowship and unity in the years to come.

Working the Devices

The plowman needs his plow. Digging by hand in the dirt will not cover much ground. Tools are required for progress and the tools of the missionary for the schedule building process are the many modes of communication available. While every individual missionary has a favorite "tool" because it has garnered the greater results, the best methodology is to wisely utilize everything in one's arsenal.[11]

The Body

The body may certainly be regarded as the most profitable tool; after all, the field won't plow itself. If the missionary is to reach the intended mark, allowing the "owners" of the plots of the field to personally meet the workman seeking for labor will often open their grounds for plowing. This is the face-to-face approach.

Physically standing before a church leader, shaking hands, and making a connection, however quick the interaction, often pays dividends for scheduling. Opportunities to accomplish this present themselves in the form of pastoral fellowships, mission's focused meetings (state, regional, and national), and attending a church service where, on certain occasions, the missionary will receive time to corporately share his calling and heart to those in the audience. By involving oneself in such events, what tends to resonate in the thought-process of a pastor is the seriousness of the missionary and the like-mindedness between the two.

---

11. It is important to note, I am in no way discounting the power of God to provide through prayer. Ultimately, He is the One Who builds the schedule, but He will not work in the place of a lazy servant. The missionary works the fields, the Lord causes the fruit of his labor to grow.

A pastor's heart is to support missionary work that will provide fruit. A good investment in a trustworthy vessel. Understandably so, as anything less than the expectation of fruit is a misuse of God's money. Therefore, a missionary that is present and making personal connections can instill confidence in church leadership.

While partaking in these fellowships, a necessary aggression is required for doors to open. If the missionary's expectation is that a mass of church leaders will flock to his display table (or wherever the missionary is positioned), he is in for a rude awakening. The necessary aggression required is when the missionary wisely and delightfully interjects themselves into the presence of pastoral leadership with a prayer card in hand, a short introduction, and, if no further follow-up questions present themselves, a polite request for a business card in return. This ensures they have seen the missionary, spoken with him, and, at least for a short while, remember him that, when he calls to follow-up, he is fresh in the pastor's mind.

The owners of the plots want laborers, but they also want the best of the lot. Men and women that will bountifully provide fruit for their church investment. As God has called, present oneself as Christ's choice servant to tend the land accordingly.

Networking

The chance to form pivotal relationships abound when the Lord is at work and the missionary is cognizant. When I was called into missions, my personal connections were practically nil. I was saved at twenty and the only Baptist church I had ever attended was my sending church based in South Florida, a location which is rather far away from strongly churched areas. As I was praying for meetings, I commenced by inquiring for opportunities in the wisest spot possible: My pastor. Whether many or few, every church leader has certain connections that the missionary can call and drop his name to open doors. This gives momentum to fill dates and creates a proximity of location to search for more.

Establishing connections within fellowships is also vital in reaping opportunities. When I was undergoing the approval process for my mission board, a certain pastor was on my committee that had helped establish a large, growing Baptist church network. I believe it was of the Lord to place this specific individual before me because I was then able to also receive endorsement through this network. Without having to personally meet or go through lengthy processes to schedule a church, I could simply inform a pastor that I was endorsed and, often times, this led to immediate scheduling. The network was trusted and the missionaries had undergone a vetting process; therefore, church leadership could have confidence for those endorsed therein. This added an extra element, on top of my mission board connections, to gain meetings.

The missionary also ought to make it a common practice to request of a pastor in a church they have presented in for personal contacts. Churches in the area and beyond that have a heart for the Lord and missions. By contacting them and revealing that a certain individual had given his recommendation, there is often a peace that the missionary is both capable and trustworthy as church leadership will not flippantly give the names of his friends if he has no belief or confidence in the individual. This same methodology works with fellow missionaries. Friendships often blossom while on the road and communicating with one another about various ministries lends to further scheduling opportunities. If a missionary has been blessed, they want their friends to reap of that fountain. Both are climbing the mountain of deputation together; a hand to reach the next ledge is a needful blessing.

There is a certain level of trust in networks. When missionaries present in churches and form relationships, their name spreads either positively or negatively. Missionaries talk. Pastors talk. It is in this network of communication and fellowship that will either greatly benefit or impede progress. Maintain a positive presence, form relationships, and utilize those connections to reach the field.

The Missionary Packet

If the missionary does not have a personal connection with a specific pastor (and sometimes even if he does), the first request he will often receive is to send his missionary packet. This is a thorough, but concise folder with specific information regarding the missionary and country of calling. It is of utmost importance to configure a packet that is pleasing to the eye and appetizing to the spirit because it plays a vital role in scheduling opportunities.

Before a pastor opens a packet, he witnesses its design. With the plethora he has received, his eye is more likely to fall upon the one that is aesthetically pleasing and features unique characteristics. What stands out visually often piques the interest of the consumer. It is this sensory element that product designers aim to capitalize on when selling their goods. Customers value appealing design and, in the instance of a missionary, one is attempting to "sell" his product to church leadership. "Well, that's not spiritual! Decisions ought to be made on the content within, not on the shiny wrapping!" True, but no decisions are being made based on shiny wrapping; rather, it is simply the element that attracts the customer to at least explore its contents. It is catching the eye before captivating the heart.

Take for example a man in leadership who has two separate missionary packets on their desk. One is highly decorative in graphic design and is appealing to the eye; whereas, the other is placed inside of a manila envelope. It may very well be possible that the missionary whose packet is inside the envelope has a better track record, more background experience, and a stronger testimony, but the pastor will usually open the aesthetically pleasing one first. This may not seem a great matter with only two packets involved because the other will still most likely receive review, even if it is in a manila envelope. What happens though if we add to his stack ten more? Or twenty? Or even one hundred? Suddenly, the missionary with a profound background finds his material muddled underneath the bunch. Yes, God's grace will open doors, but it is wise for the missionary to not make a difficult job even more strenuous. Working with a graphic designer will increase the visibility of the missionary and does not have to break the bank. An aesthetically pleasing packet will often help in getting a foot in the door, the contents will usually determine whether one is welcomed inside.

Have you ever purchased a jar of sauce from the grocery store because of its visual design, only to find the flavor of its contents were not worthy of human consumption? The missionary packet ought never match that experience. The contents within must complement or exceed those without. With elevated expectations from the packaging, the pastor wants a flavor worthy of his time. By delivering details of the country of calling and of the missionary himself, a desirable flavor can be achieved in two distinct ways:

(1) Thorough and Concise: "In the beginning God created the heavens and the earth..." This short sentence tells the reader a surplus of information in only ten words. God is eternal, supreme, and the Creator for which all that is finds its source in Him. Without detailing the specifications of Himself and the intricate shaping of created things, the reader is made acutely aware of what is. The Word is both thorough (complete and containing all necessary details) and concise (All the needed words are contained without over-embellishment). In essence, everything the Lord deemed is needful for any individual to know is founded within His Word; there is no holy appendix or bonus material available. Why is this important to a missionary packet? The packet is not purposed to be a book. A pastor's time is precious; therefore, when he reviews it he wants to gain as much information as possible in as brief a time as possible. Rather than intricately detailing every facet of one's life, salvation,

ministry, education, experience, and calling, a short snip or a quick gaze ought to suffice. If a church leader is unable to reap the information in a timely manner and as a result, either in frustration, disinterest, and/or the hustle and bustle of ministry, lays the packet to the side, chances are slim he will review it again. Maintaining a thorough and concise packet of information is the first major ingredient to having delicious content.

(2) Relevant and Trustworthy: If you have ever had a chance to review job applications, certain factors tend to stand out. Applicants tend to over-embellish their abilities and even add unnecessary, irrelevant skill sets and experiences. I have heard of one applicant who even climaxed his cover letter by stating, "Please realize I am not a braggart or conceited." The list goes on and on as individuals attempt to grasp at any relevant key word or modicum of excellence to convince the employer that they are worthy to be hired. Unfortunately, these very reasons are why many remain on the market. We try not to come across as braggarts, but our résumé wreaks of self-glorification. The reality is that the employer, or the pastor in the missionary's case, almost always learns the truth. Please do not misunderstand, I am not stating to withhold facts and accomplishments. Include all of the wonderful works the Lord Jesus has performed through oneself, but know that it was only through Him that anything was ever accomplished and through Him that the pastor will be convicted. There is no need to provide "overkill." Regardless of whether the missionary has a long or short list to transcribe, write what is relevant and write what is true; the Lord will make the flavor sweet in the pastor's mouth.

The missionary packet that opens doors is pleasing to the sight and appetizing to the soul. It does not perform the entire work, but it is the silent workhorse on the pastor's desk until the necessary time to review. It is up to the missionary himself to determine whether or not the flavors are able to be digested or spit out.

Email, Telephone, and Social Media

If you have never personally experienced the long hours attributed to cold calling, deputation will transform any novice into a master. Communicating with church leadership may be rocky at the outset, but the more one converses the quicker the missionary will catch their stride. I remember when I initially was contacting churches that I had a word document open on my computer with set phraseology for leaving voicemails and answering questions that I might fail to recall because of my nervous jitters. Between my phone conversations and my less than stellar emails, I can only say it was fully the grace of the Lord that we especially had any bookings early on!

Reaping the benefits of communication devices demands long hours of hard work with little, but integral reward. Unless the missionary has a familial history in evangelistic ministry (and even that has limits), personal contacts and connections will run out. Arriving on the field usually requires a vast amount of church support; therefore, there is going to be a demand to contact unknown pastors from unknown churches. It is important to note, every missionary has a different format and procedure that best fits their personality and yields the greatest results. While one missionary may rarely receive a returned email, another might schedule the majority of churches through this type of communication. What I suggest is that each individual find what best suits them, but also partake in all aspects of device communication. The more that is distributed, the more return is received.

The process of emailing churches is often both the most comfortable method and the first line of communication. Many pastors will request an email with the missionary's packet and other information for their inspection. What makes email so profitable is that a massive number can be sent in a short period of time and any available facts and attachments can be included. I have a missionary friend that gathered many church emails into one spreadsheet and was able to send out mass email blasts, which yielded for him many positive replies. Email is basically a one-stop shop for any church to receive all of the relevant information they would require in evaluating a missionary. It may introduce the individual, the sending church, any possible connections, dates of availability, relevant contact information, and needful attachments. Often times this serves as a precursor to a hopeful coming conversation for scheduling. The missionary ought to record the day the email was sent and plan a follow-up call 1-3 weeks ahead.

The follow-up call (or cold call) can be one of the more strenuous exercises of deputation. It can feel as if it is a lot of work with little pay. What is important to remember is that little pay is better than no pay and, on certain occasions, one may be surprised with rather large returns. When calling churches, the missionary ought to be prepared for an answer on the end of the line, whether it be a receptionist, a staff member, or the pastor himself. While every conversation has its nuances, it is important to have the ability to "read the air" when communicating. Is the individual busy or willing to talk? Is he willing to invite you in? Are you asked questions about your background, call, or doctrine? Is the church able to support new missionaries? Giving simple, clear, and concise answers and politely asking questions will assist the missionary in maintaining focus and the pastor (or staff member) in positively receiving what is stated and requested. If interest is peaked, a greater possibility to schedule a date is afforded. I had personally reaped the majority of my remaining appointments by contacting pastors and churches personally over the phone, but I spent long hours for months on end. By the time I was halfway through deputation, I never wanted to make another call! Again, while every missionary has varying results from differing methods, I had personally found that if I could actually speak with a pastor on the phone, there was a greater chance of receiving a booking. Furthermore, many of these opportunities made over the phone derived from following ministry friends online.

Social media is a prime medium for opening doors. As travel commences and relationships are built, pastors and missionary friends will usually stay in touch online. These individuals will have contacts which are not currently in one's phone list. By performing a quick search through various social media friends/followers or observing missionary post updates, one can take note of new pastors to reach out to in the coming days. This is very similar to the networking section above because it is utilizing formed relationships to open doors to present in the future. Furthermore, a church may not always have a website, but they often have a social media presence. By browsing online and taking note of godly, likeminded churches, there is a reaping to be had. When it is thoroughly utilized, the missionary can gain many presentation dates scheduled.

The simple truth of the matter is that the greater the number of churches one can present will usually reap the most support gained. These three devices, when properly utilized, will fill the remaining dates of the travel calendar for presenting the call and raising funds. It may seem like a lot of labor in the fields for only a small reaping, but the Lord will bless the hard work of His missionary. Press on toward the mark.

Where and Who Do I Schedule?

"Will I really have to travel to the other side of the United States? Will the church take us on?" Both questions have one main, general answer: Maybe. How the Lord leads every missionary is according to His personal and divine will, but His servant can rest assured that He will not "waste time."

In regard to travel, many missionaries trek whatever distance is necessary when an opportunity presents itself. Before I commenced deputation, I was told by missionary friends that they had once spanned the entire United States, from California to New York, in one week for two separate conferences. My mind was boggled by such a trip! I did not even enjoy a drive to the grocery store, how was I going to I survive the upcoming time on the road? I soon found that the Lord gave grace; even for operating a vehicle. When I once loathed the thought of sitting behind the wheel for any significant amount of time, I was quickly able to tune out those feelings and focus on other matters. Instead of driving remaining as a dreadful demand of deputation, it was *usually* a quiet and peaceful endeavor. Suffice it to say, I never had to span the United States. When scheduling churches, I strove to remain within certain regions as often as possible.

Regional and continental scheduling are not in opposition, but each missionary will attempt to pattern their travels more with one over the other. Regional scheduling is the process of booking several church meetings over a set period of time within a specific region. This is the method most missionaries prefer, but often the most difficult to accomplish. It requires the hard labor of contacting a multitude of pastors in a smaller circumference until the schedule is filled. Continental scheduling is the process of booking several church meetings over a set period of time in multiple regions of the United States. This allows the missionary to expand their perimeter's reach of contacts, but may demand the missionary serve as a pinball on the road as they travel thousands of miles in multiple directions over short timeframes for elongated periods. The former is more difficult at the outset, but provides the comforts from road weariness. The latter is easier to build a schedule, but more wearying during travel. While nearly every missionary will experience to some extent both regional and continental scheduling, the question the missionary has to ask himself is, "Where would I rather perform the <u>harder</u> labor... on the phones or on the roads?" Regardless of one's answer, put in the work in the fields and allow the Lord to bring His increase, wherever that increase is secured.

The question of "who" when booking is rather personal and specifics are more difficult to distinguish. Every pastor and church is different and each path the Lord leads the missionary is unique. This section ought to be coupled with the above section entitled "The Representative Mouthpiece." The missionary ought to present in churches that maintain a like-mindedness in faith and practice. Yet, rather than repeat what has already been stated, further remarks can be made on identifying a better "who" opportunity from a lesser one. In fact, I would like to present a word of caution for missionaries. While finally receiving an invite to present at a church may appear as water in a time of drought, beware of accepting every invitation. There are certain ministries that simply book missionaries with no intention of blessing them or taking them on. Usually these take the form of phone conversations or questionnaires where either very little is asked of the missionary's beliefs and background or there are a large number of critical questions. Remember, these cases are usually rare as many pastors and ministries love missions and missionaries, but there are occurrences to be wary of. If a missionary does wind up presenting in such a church, be a light and a delight. God will bless even in frustrating circumstances.

A good "who" opportunity is when a missionary has heard through the grapevine on the profound mission's heart of a church family. When a pastor and church is known for missions, one can expect great blessings when presenting amongst them and then flowing forth thereafter. Pray and strive for the Lord to open a door for a meeting with these ministries. If the opportunity is an unknown church, take note of the flow of the conversation; as stated above. Though this is a touchy subject and certain individuals may disagree, I believe the following to be worthwhile. While it ought never be the desire of any missionary to reschedule a church meeting, one must know that there are certain times when a wishy-washy ministry has been scheduled and if a wonderful opportunity presents itself with a mission's loving church on the same date, the missionary will have to make a decision on whether to reconsider the initial scheduling. Again, rescheduling is never the goal or the desire, but the truth of the matter is that there are certain churches simply bringing in multiple missionaries with no intention of blessing them or taking them on. Learn to read the landscape and pray to the Lord for a decision of peace.

Whether regional or continental, a better or lesser opportunity, the Lord gives grace. Know who He has made the missionary and his family to be, give Him glory for the opportunities He presents in one's path, and push forward in His power.

Summary Remarks

Ploughing a field and building a presentation schedule contain roughly the same labor; they are both preparing the ground for planting and harvest. It is this hard work of seeking plots to labor in that often feels the most unrewarding, but, as William Carey declared, to continue straightly, set the eyes on the definitive mark. Do not take one's hand off of the plow, do not set one's eyes on discouraging plots of soil; rather, keep oneself directed on Christ and the field He has called one to harvest. In His time, the ploughing will cease and the sowing will commence.

Chapter 4
Missionary Communication in the Local Church

We have all heard of those blessed with a "green thumb." Individuals that are innately endowed with the ability to reap the richest, most bountiful harvests of the ground. It is clear that these individuals have coupled that God-given gift with tender love and increased understanding in their craft to maximize the production of abundance in plant life. While not every seed will yield fruit, they have learned to diminish potential loss. The contrast of a green thumb is a black thumb. It is founded in one completely incapable of properly nourishing plant life. These individuals can transform even a lush garden into a wasteland in record timing. They are not only ungifted with tending to the soil, but they have also failed to adequately research and apply the proper maintenance of distinct plants to make up for their own shortcomings. Though they may try and try again, the planted seeds reap little to no fruit.

What good is a plowed field if the workman is incapable of properly planting and tending the seed unto the production of a harvest? The soil was prepared for the sole intent of reaping gain! In a world of green and black thumbs, a missionary must strive to have a "green thumb." A green thumb missionary is one that has learned to couple the calling of God with the learned wisdom of his craft unto a full harvest of fruit. A busy deputation schedule is worthless if the individual cannot reap a harvest. Rather than cultivate life, their black thumb tends to tear up the soil and uproot the plants. They not only have nothing of worth to add unto the congregation, but they also do great harm. No strengthening in the faith, no conviction unto action, no moving of the power of the Lord. Though they may present the ministry over and again, they continually struggle to yield anything of worth in the labor fields of the local church.

How does this occur? Can a missionary that is called by God truly have a "black thumb?" Unfortunately, it happens far more often than one may believe. The overwhelming difference between missionaries with green and black thumbs is often centered in their ability to either communicate effectively or not. One retired pastor wrote in regard to ineffective missionary communication:

> I became very frustrated with both the missionary presentations and the messages they preached. Our church loved missionaries, but endured their presentations and messages. More and more of my pastor friends were no longer allowing missionaries to preach in their church because they were not effective communicators. Pastors would schedule missionaries for their missions conference, but have a pastor friend preach at the conference instead of the missionaries. Pastors also limited the time a missionary could give a presentation and that time kept going down! Missionary question and answer sessions were eliminated because they were not effective. The lack of

101

effective communication from missionaries caused less and less pastors to even want a missionary in their church. The end result - it was taking longer and longer for missionaries to raise the funds to get to the mission field.[12]

What a profound statement. The reality is such that the cumulative effect of ineffective missionary speakers has wrought a falling away from supporting new missionaries. If the workman is to expect a bounty in the labor fields of America, he must strive for a green thumb; capable of reaping through the planting and tending of the goodly seed through effective communication.

Effective Biblical Communication of the Missionary

Some years ago, my wife and I had the opportunity to visit the Pearl Harbor Memorial. We witnessed the many sights and watched the tribute video play as we learned of our nation's history. Our hearts were moved by what our eyes witnessed. As we continued our tour around the memorial, there were certain stone structures set with various carved quotations upon them. One of them contained President Franklin D. Roosevelt's words from the famous Fireside Chats. He declared, "We are now in this war. We are all in it - all the way. Every single man, woman, and child is a partner in the most tremendous undertaking of our American history." Flowing from that day's experiences, his very words at that moment seemed to reverberate off the stone so

---

12. Lewis McClendon, E-mail to Nick Zarrella, July 7, 2021.

intensely that we completely understood how those brave soldiers of our history were convicted to action.

Such must be the communication of the missionary. One must maintain the ability to transmit the burden of Christ's work unto the people in such a way that they are brought under the conviction of the Holy Spirit to action. Through the use of modern communication programs, visual tools and, most importantly, one's own mouthpiece, the missionary can profoundly shake the foundations of the congregation, not simply on an emotional level, but unto the depths of their heart spiritually. Through effective communication in power of the Holy Spirit of the Living God, a mighty and convicting work can be accomplished.

Effective Communication is not Eloquent Speech (Exodus 4:10-12)

A grave misunderstanding in effective communication is the belief that a missionary is required to have eloquent lips. While eloquence is a wonderful trait that ought to be refined, it is not the prescription for biblical, effective communication.

When the Lord was giving the charge unto Moses to return to Egypt and speak unto Pharaoh as His medium for the release of His people, one of the excuses he gave unto the Lord was his lack of eloquence. He told the Lord that he had never developed advanced oratory skills even unto that very day; rather, he claimed he was actually slow of speech and tongue. These words hold the idea of a thickening, a hardness, an implacability. He was stating that he has never been able to speak with influence and eloquence and the situation was impossible to be resolved. There might have been a certain truth to his words. Despite having been educated in the wisdom of the Egyptians (Acts 7:22a), it is possible that he had not displayed any real development or progression in his ability to speak publicly. Whatever the case, the Lord was in control.

God, in His omniscience, questioned Moses' own knowledge. Yes, he may have been educated in the wisdom of Egypt and possibly even displayed a lack of eloquence, but the Lord is both the Maker of man's mouth and of those that are deaf, dumb, seeing, and blind. He intricately understands the capability of each man and, more so, how He can utilize even those that are lacking in certain abilities. Therefore, He again charges Moses to "go," and promised that He Himself would be with Moses' mouth to teach him the words to say. This is a vital concept to comprehend for the missionary. The life of Moses exhibits a man that, when absent of the power of God, was unable to overcome his own shortcomings. It was only when the Lord spoke through Him that he was able and capable to move the masses through words and deeds (Acts 7:22b). It was God's Word spoken through him that had power. Alone he was incapable, but the Lord opened his mouth and gave unto him spiritual utterance to speak the words and accomplish the work.

Eloquence means nothing if God is not in it, but if God is in it, eloquence is not a required trait. While it is a wonderful quality, it is not the definition of biblical, effective communication. If a missionary is going to effectively communicate, God must be with his words. Eloquence varies from individual to individual. Though it can be learned and ought to be continually refined, the Lord has gifted some with the ability of an Apollos and others that are as Paul. It was not their eloquence which had power, but God's presence and their knowledge in His Word.

Effective Communication is not Emotional Stimulation (Acts 19:21ff)

"Great is Diana of the Ephesians! ... Great is Diana of the Ephesians!" Remember this account from Acts 19? When the silversmith's finances and the false god of Diana were in danger of loss and rejection, they turned the city into an emotional uproar. Everyone shouted this phrase during a passionate tirade that lasted for a period of two hours. After the outcry was complete because the people were confronted by the town clerk, the entire assembly dismissed. Even the absolute height of emotional chaos could only last two hours.

The issue with emotional stimulation is that it is brief, it has an expiration date. Yet we know that God gave people emotions. Stimulating them does maintain a defined part in effective communication; therefore, touching videos and emotional stories which stir the heart are needful, but they are not enough to sustain the ministry as they only last upwards of "two hours." They are swiftly fleeting. Relying on them as the ultimate factor for effective communication is then setting the ministry on unsteady ground. Once they have dissipated (and they will dissipate), whatever connections existed between the missionary's emotionally stirring presentation and their heart will be severed and the church will fall back into its former state. Feelings are fickle and ever-changing

105

because, once the "town clerk" arrives, the people will quickly disband.

The goal of effective communication is not founded in fleeting emotional stimulation, but the sustained conviction of Christ. Hudson Taylor once wrote to his mother requesting her for prayer. He had suffered problems and issues and difficulties and perplexities, which had battled against him and his emotions. In the midst of that letter, he stated, "had not the Lord been specially gracious to me, as not my mind been sustained by the conviction that the work is His and that He is with me in what it is no empty figure to call 'the thick of the conflict.'"[13] It was the sustained conviction founded in Christ that pushed him forward in faithful service, despite extreme circumstances and trivialities.

The congregation has to be moved to conviction in Christ. He is the Sustainer even when residing in the "thick of the conflict," pushing the congregation forward to carry on the work. Yes, show the videos and tell the stories, but emphasize and entrust the work upon the Word of Christ Jesus, which is able to pierce, not only the emotions of the heart, but the very soul of man.

Effective Communication is Biblical Communication (2 Corinthians 11:6)

When Adoniram Judson had opportunity to preach to

---

13. Taylor, Frederick Howard. Taylor Geraldine. *Hudson Taylor's Spiritual Secret.* S.l.: Benediction Classics, 2020.

a large gathering in the States after spending many years abroad in Burma, much to the dismay of the crowd he preached the Gospel. His wife, who had been questioned by several disappointed listeners as to why he chose that subject for his speaking, mentioned of Dr. Judson the complaints. The conversation is as follows:

> "Why, what do they want?" He inquired; "I presented the most interesting subject in the world, to the best of my ability." "But they wanted something different - a story." "Well, I am sure I gave them a story - the most thrilling one that can be conceived of." "But they had it before. They wanted something new of a man who had just come from the antipodes." "Then I am glad they have it to say, that a man coming from the antipodes had nothing better to tell than the wondrous story of Jesus' dying love."[14]

Therein stands the difficulty of recognizing and fighting the urge to appease the human heart. People like stories. They want to hear about something new, something captivating. Again, there is nothing wrong with the telling of personal experiences of the world abroad and how the Lord Jesus has worked a great and mighty work, but personal stories have no power intrinsically tied to them. Dr. Judson understood that truth. The strength for piercing even unto the dividing asunder of the soul and spirit is solely founded in the Word of God (Hebrews 4:12). It is dependent on the skillful, Spirit-filled transmission of His Word (one's biblical communication), which will determine how effective the missionary's communication truly is.

---

14. Anderson, Courtney. *To the Golden Shore: The Life of Adoniram Judson.* Valley Forge: Judson Press, 1987.

While writing to the Corinthian church, Paul was warning the congregation to beware of falling into the snare of a false Gospel. Subtle words from false prophets had attempted to infiltrate the hearts of the people and Paul wanted the church members to reject them and their message. It is then in verse 6 where he makes a claim that may be somewhat surprising for an individual seeking to improve their communication skills: *"But though I be rude in speech..."* Paul was rude in speech? How could a man that could write with such a skillful hand be unskilled in the field of public speaking? While he did have some ongoing health issues, it is surprising to note his humility in communication. Yet, there is an all-important caveat. He continued his thought by writing, *"But though I be rude in speech, yet not in knowledge..."* That is a significant charge to the missionary seeking to effectively communicate. Paul was not eloquent nor a capable storyteller, but he was knowledgeable. He had a thorough comprehension of the Word and will and way of the Lord and was able to communicate it effectively based on that intimate understanding.

Effective communication is biblical communication. It is the transmission of God's Word by God's power for God's sustaining conviction. He utilizes the Moses's, the Judson's, the Paul's... Yes, His lowly servants to effectually and mightily relay His Word to people. When He is with one's mouth, all manner of His Word, whether in the States or in the antipodes, is able to be uttered unto convicting action. Let us look at some biblical missionary examples of developing or utilizing effective communication.

The Son in the Faith (Philippians 2:19-23)

Timothy was a powerful force for the missionary ministry. His life speaks on the blessedness of discipleship for practically, biblically, and effectively serving in ministry. The Apostle Paul, entering into Derbe and Lystra, highly regarded the young man for his love and knowledge of Christ. The Bible details that he was a man well-reported of (Acts 16:2) and that he had a strong faith since his infancy (2 Timothy 3:15). When Paul addressed the Philippians, he greatly commended Timothy unto them.

Timothy was to be a source of comfort. Paul was hopeful to hear of the Philippian's good state in Christ; thus, he had no better representative to report than this young man. He told the church that Timothy was *as a son with the father.* This father/son relationship was not biological, but spiritual. The two were so much alike that Paul said they were of the same mind/spirit. This spiritual relationship transpired over the course of the years of their traveling as Timothy was discipled into the likeness of Christ by him. He learned of the work, the will, the way, and the Word more deeply under his tutelage. He soon became a proven man, having served alongside Paul in the Gospel.

Could Timothy have strengthened the church in Philippi if he was not able to effectively communicate the truth? Definitely not. Paul had spent significant time discipling this young man. It was over the course of the years of his development that he was sometimes sent as a short-term representative to certain local churches. This was practical training for him, especially in the area of communication. One of the more difficult tests was when he

109

was sent to Corinth. Paul told the believers there that Timothy would *"bring you into remembrance of my ways which be in Christ, as I teach every where in every church."* (1 Corinthians 4:17) It is interesting that Paul's preaching and teaching were emphasized as the basis of effectively communicating unto churches, while his work was highlighted as the proof of his ministry (16:10). It was the words that had the power, and the works that proved them. The Corinthian believers had a nasty habit of disregarding the works of Paul and questioning his leadership role in Apostolic office, but they could not contend with his words sourced in the Word of God. What would happen to the lesser-known Timothy before this harsh congregation? They might be able to deny his works, but if they had potential to strip the boldness from him, they could silence his mouth from preaching the truth. Therefore, Paul encouraged them to receive Timothy gladly as a workman of the Lord. In this manner, Timothy was able to learn that in whatsoever place he found himself, whether it was encouraging or not, he had to maintain speaking the word of the Lord. It was God's Word spoken through His choice servants which were utilized to strengthen local churches. Therefore, they had to be effectively communicated before the people.

Paul would continue to mentor his son in the faith. In the epistles of 1 and 2 Timothy, he instructed him on leading a church, to be devoted to reading and knowing the Word, to pursue after the Lord and His righteousness, to beware of false teachers, and to be approved in the eyes of the Lord. Timothy continually grew in his wisdom of Christ, thus his opportunities increased. Where he started as a promising missionary traveling companion, he was soon sent as Paul's representative to local churches, and later he became a lead pastor over a congregation in Ephesus only to finally raise up the flag of the faith as the days of Paul were nearing their end. All of this was possible in Christ because of those who invested their lives in teaching him the Word that he might be profitable unto the Lord in the ministry.

Discipleship in the Word is the crucial need for missionary work. Many can perform with their hands, but their mouth is unable to speak effectively because they have a limited knowledge of Scripture. As Timothy was discipled in Scripture by his family, his church, and his spiritual father; likewise, the missionary must have a depth of training in the Word if one is to communicate effectively.

Telling by the Mouth (Acts 15:22-32)

After a conclusion was reached at the Jerusalem Council and Paul and Barnabas were returning to Antioch, Judas and Silas were sent alongside them from the church of Jerusalem as representatives to relay the conclusion. Within the letter sent unto the church at Antioch, the leaders in Jerusalem wrote that Judas and Silas would, *"tell you the same things by mouth."* As representatives of their church, it was vital for them to have a proficiency of speaking through their knowledge of Scripture to relay the necessary information for which they were entrusted.

When they arrived at the church and read the epistolary conclusion from the council, Judas and Silas arose and exhorted the brethren with many words, confirming them; being prophets themselves. Considering that they were leaders within the Jerusalem church, it is possible they held the office of a Prophet, which has ceased today. Regardless, they also clearly exhibited the spiritual gift of prophecy (communicating God's Word; forthtelling), evidenced by their ability to address the congregation with conclusive words from the council that were able to encourage, appeal to, and strengthen the brethren.

While they relayed the conclusion of the council and assuredly spoke the truth of the Word, it is clear that the preaching and exhortation of Judas and Silas was filled with the power of God unto the edifying of the church. They were able to effectively communicate the Word that the church was able to stand alongside of them in agreement. This is critical because it was not merely their faithfulness in service for which the church in Jerusalem sent them, but because they were gifted and able to speak the Word by mouth. If they were faithful workers, but incapable communicators; they would not have been worthy representatives. It was their effective communication that set the church at rest in the will and ways of God, and the words and works of Silas which evidenced the calling of God upon him as a missionary.

The Articulate Apollos (Acts 18:24ff)

A prime example of the need for biblical training for missionary work is taken from Apollos. Unlike Paul, he was eloquent, but lacking the full depth of Scriptural knowledge. He was a man defined by his proficient oration, his love for God, his fervent spirit, and his teaching ability, but he was sorely lacking because he only knew of the baptism of John.

While he was in Ephesus, he was speaking in the synagogue when Aquila and Priscilla overheard him. Recognizing his qualities and passion, but also his lack of knowledge in the fullness of the truth, they took him to the side and *"expounded unto him the way of God more perfectly."* The two disciples recognized the spirit and love for God in Apollos, therefore, they sought to explain the fullness of the way of Christ unto him. What is then made clear in the Text is that, after his time of discipleship, he set his sights on future works. Having heard of the congregation at Corinth, Apollos departed to water the ground where Paul had sown. Priscilla and Aquilla, seemingly in agreement, sent him with a letter that the church in Corinth receive him. His purpose was then concluded in vv. 27-28 stating they he was going to aid the believers (a form of strengthening) and to continue to convince the Jews of Christ through the Scriptures.

The unique account of Apollos displays the need for discipleship unto the knowledge of the perfect way founded in Scripture. Though he was eloquent and learned and full of vigor, he was sorely lacking in the most crucial area and thus was incapable of effectively communicating the Word unto the aid of churches. It was only when he was set aside from the work and discipled in the more perfect way, that a local church was able to recommend him and another receive him unto the strengthening of the ministry.

Paul commanded Timothy to *"preach the Word, be instant in season, out of season; reprove, rebuke, exhort with all longsuffering and doctrine,"* and for Titus to *"speak thou the things which become sound doctrine."* He encouraged Silas to strengthen the churches and for Apollos to water where he had sown. The Word of God is where the missionary's communication receives power. As Paul declared, *"But though I be rude in speech, yet not in knowledge..."* If the missionary is incapable of strengthening a church, it is not because his tongue is slow or his oratory skills lack eloquence, rather it is because he has not spent the necessary efforts to establish a working knowledge of the Scriptures. When the biblical missionaries spoke the Word of God, the people were confirmed. Why? They intimately knew it. They were deeply involved in learning, comprehending, and receiving it into their very being. Apollos was so learned that the Bible states he *"mightily convinced the Jews, and that publickly, shewing by the Scriptures that Jesus was the Christ."* They were overwhelmed by his knowledge. Effective missionary communication has the power to shake the very soul into conformity with Christ.

As churches were strengthened by visiting missionaries in the Bible, there remains the urgent need today. Modern-day pastors cannot be frustrated with missionaries. Churches cannot simply endure them and their presentations. If the individual is incapable of clearly transmitting their call and His Word because of ineffective communication, the work of the Lord will not be efficiently and effectively accomplished. If the laborer cannot strengthen his fellow workmen, how will he reap in the foreign harvest fields? What fruit will be unto the church's account? Which foreign saints will greet them? The Bible is clear that effective communication is an integral part of the deputation ministry; therefore, it must find precedence in the life of the missionary today. As God is calling missionaries to the field, it is the duty of the workman to serve as a worthy representative.

Modern-Day Expectations for Missionary Communication

Connecting the Scriptural expectations of the missionary with the modern-day is not so much as building a bridge as it is expanding on the biblical principles for the contemporary audience. The difficulty in such a task is found in that while the Bible and the culture therein is unchanging, the society of today is in constant motion. There are ebbs and flows as the winds of change sweep the land with new personalities and viewpoints. Some of what is written today regarding "modern" expectations of communication may not find acceptance in the modernity of coming generations. There will be biblical practices and principles in the following section that must remain consistent, but cultural trends or adaptations that may not. Therefore, I will attempt to balance the many general and specific principles that this section might remain as timeless as possible.

It cannot be understated that the missionary has certain expectations placed upon them by pastors and local churches. Deputation can be a sort of "proving ground" for watchful leadership as they inspect and expect a certain level of capability when one is communicating and interacting with a church family. The purpose of this section is to assist the missionary in navigating the path of pleasing God, remaining true to oneself before the Lord, and being mindful of fulfilling the expectations of local churches.

Pastoral Expectations

It is not a secret that pastors have been frustrated with the communication (in)abilities of visiting missionaries. Though there is the want and desire to support missions and send those that are called to the various parts of the globe, churches are also wanting to partner with capable and well-trained individuals. Those that have displayed a knowledge of the Word and the ability to effectively proclaim it to an audience. One pastor, in reference to missionaries needing communication training, stated,

> The reason this training is important is because the pastor is being judged by his people off of the decision to invite a capable or incapable communicator; especially when communicating the Gospel is the heart of missions. Another reason this training is important is because, in most of the average church member's mind, pastors and missionaries are professionals and there are professionals sitting in the pews listening to a so-called "professional" communicate. That communication does not have to be perfect, but it cannot be sloppy.[15]

Within a Pastor's mind flows the judgment of his people alongside the desire to impart a mission's heart into his congregation. He understands that they must fulfill the Great Commission mandate on the local church, which is accomplished through partnering with missionaries. The missionary's effectiveness, or lack thereof, in communication will spread and portray either a positive or negative outlook. One must not allow for the humiliation of a pastor, the ridicule of missionaries, nor the embarrassment of one's

---

15. Tom Hunter, Personal Interview, July 7, 2021.

representation of Christ and His calling through lackluster, sloppy, ineffective communication.

Pastoral expectations come in a variety of general and specific areas for which every church leader desires to see accomplished. The missionary must understand that, as an invited guest, they are to serve as a representative of Christ and the pastor of the local church. One must be capable and ready to extend the mission's heart of the Lord <u>and</u> the pastor upon the congregation. The invitation to present is not an opportunity to sell oneself or to "bludgeon" the people over specific or general deficiencies; rather, it is to strengthen the people to missional action.

Intra-Pulpit Communication

Standing in the pulpit of an unknown pastor amongst a sea of unrecognizable faces can be daunting and exhilarating. One might feel like Martin Luther when he stood in fear of his life before Emperor Charles the V in Worms, "Here I stand. I can do no other. God help me! Amen." The missionary desires to bless and encourage and do a fine job representing Christ and his call, but the cry of the heart is simply "God... help me!" That's the right place to start. Without Him, all is pointless.

Intra-pulpit communication is the most vital aspect of a missionary visit. There is authority when one stands on holy ground and proclaims all that God has reserved through the tongue and life of the missionary for the people. By recognizing the Lord's power and preparing practically for the presentation, the missionary can mightily impact the church for the fulfilling of His work in the Great Commission.

The Presentation Video

As Jeremiah witnessed first-hand the tragic state of the city and people of Jerusalem, he cried out the words, *"Mine eye affecteth mine heart"* (Lamentations 3:51). It was the direct visuals that caused a great burden to overflow within him and then the Word that he sought as he lamented for the Lord to renew His people as in former days. A missionary presentation video is not a movie preview, a landscape and wildlife promo, or media entertainment. One is not aiming to make the people believe that such and such a place is where they ought to plan their next great vacation. The goal of the video is that the heart of the congregation is so intimately stirred for lost souls that they are compelled to cry out unto God, as Jeremiah had, for His redemptive power to penetrate the people. They have to witness the trenches of spiritual darkness that pervade the land, and then seek the Light that is able pierce it. If the eyes have moved the heart, the heart will bend the knee.

The presentation video reaps an interesting dilemma due to its ever-changing nature and audience. What once never existed, soon developed into voice recordings, then slideshows, and now (relative to the timing of this writing) into HD and 4K video. There is no telling how far technological development will proceed in the coming years. Furthermore, there are the constant changes in cultural attitudes and expectations. Until the early 2000s, twenty-minute videos were normal and gladly received, but that has long fluttered away. Peoples of the modern world (2010 to the time of this writing) have a shorter attention span and a higher expectation for visual engagements. Rather than drum through an endless slideshow of background particulars and peripheral minutia, there is an expectation to receive the needful information without the extras and fillers. Rather than tuning in to the entire story, the contemporary congregation desires to efficiently and engagingly receive only the critical pieces of information. There is also the reality that the development of a video will have varied opinions on what is and is not effective; regardless of the day and age for which one lives. The length, the content, the music, and the verbiage must all be taken into account in order to provide what is profitable to the majority of local churches in the modern-day. Therefore, the missionary will have to maintain an intimate comprehension of the ever-flowing technological advances and cultural attitudes to produce quality, professional, and acceptable material.

With all of that understood, how then can any missionary expect to appease the majority? Again, I will hearken back to Jeremiah - *"Mine eye affecteth mine heart."* That is the goal. Jesus Himself would look upon the multitudes and His heart would be moved unto compassion for their souls (Matthew 9:36-38); a compassion He also desired for His own disciples (John 4:35). Regardless of the capabilities one has in video development, if it can cause the eye to affect/move the heart unto compassion in Christ for lost souls, its purpose has been fulfilled. The following principles will assist in that endeavor:

(1) Length: The length of the video has to coincide with

the average amount of given time a missionary has to present. One does not want the majority of minutes to be overtaken by the video. Therefore, if a missionary is granted an average of 10-15 minutes (not including the time to preach), a three to five-minute video will suffice. Remember, it is the Word which has convicting power, not the visuals. Allow the video to stir the emotions of the heart. It will be the testimony and, if given opportunity, the preaching in Christ Jesus that will serve as the convicting force.

(2) Content: It is vital to remember that the missionary is not producing a travel documentary. Do not waste several precious seconds or minutes in displaying the various types of animals and local scenery if they have nothing to do with preventing the people from knowing the Lord. Rather, unveil the strongholds of religion and culture which have encapsulated them. The temples, cathedrals, rituals, festivals, trinkets, idols, and ceremonies that stand opposed to the Gospel of salvation. Show the faces and actions of the people as they partake in their daily lives and in the sin that pervades society.[16] Show the darkness in their eyes that speaks of the condition of their soul (Matthew 6:22-23). The reality is that the people filmed in the videos and the faces that are witnessed are singular evidences of the general population which are spiritually dead and on their way to hell. They are lost and in need of the Savior; something that no animal or castle or waterfall can claim.

---

16. Be very wary of adding any graphic content. While there are certain elements of society that do display the shear depravity of the people and culture, they are not always "church-friendly."

The climax of the video ought to include a charge for partaking together. As my family and I were on deputation, we utilized the catchphrase, "We for Japan, Japan for Christ." This brought about a togetherness between us and the churches. While "we" were going into the pits, that "we" also included the church members which were staying back and holding the ropes for us. "We together for Japan! Why? To reach Japan for Christ." When the video can finish with the hope of Christ and the opportunity to partner with a missionary to realize that hope in a distant land, it connects the minds of the people to their profound role in fulfilling the Great Commission.

(3) Music: There is certainly a range of music available to the missionary for what they choose to play during their presentation. While some missionaries will opt for Christian songs, others may utilize the cultural music derived from the country of calling. Personally, I have been told on multiple occasions by church members that they enjoyed the cultural music coinciding with the video. It had allowed for a more immersive experience as their ears were given a similar treatment as their eyes. Again, this is not required nor necessary, but I think it beneficial to expose the people to the sights and sounds of the foreign people.

There is also the necessity of choosing the right music for producing professional-quality videos. Rather than simply picking a good song and infusing it into the content without reckoning how the content itself coincides with the tune, the missionary ought to pick a song that can seamlessly match the video. A beat that will accompany the changing of a slide, a progressive elevation of sound that builds suspense toward the climax, etc. No, the aim is not to entertain the people, but that does not excuse poor quality or lackluster production. When the pastor of a church plays a video for special occasions and national holidays, he does not approve of something lazily thrown together. He wants quality that is stirring, profound, and well-done; such as ought to be the case with the missionary video.

(4) Verbiage: To speak, or not to speak? This is another area where there are always going to be varying viewpoints. Some prefer to have a voiceover explanation; others prefer text on the screen to do the "talking." What the missionary ought to remember is the need for professionalism in their video. For example, we have all heard those with a voice for radio. Individuals that maintain a certain quality and tone that syncs well over the airwaves. Any other type just does not seem to "fit" the prescription for radio quality and, in fact, can even distract or turn off listeners. It is similar for a missionary video. If one desires a voiceover, make sure it is a voice "for video;" otherwise it has the potential to have the opposite effect desired. Instead of holding the attention and connecting the people, it may serve as a distraction. Just as with the content and music, a voiceover has to be seamless in its quality, tone, and transitions.

On-screen text is easier to manage and can be swiftly formatted if necessary alterations are required. Such is not the case if a quality voiceover has been recorded. For example, when we first commenced deputation, the Japanese people were the largest unreached people group in the entire world. It was barely six months into our travel when the statistics were updated to then deem them as the second largest unreached. Necessary changes had to be made to coincide with the updated information, which were swiftly performed through a simple editing of the text.

While a well-done voiceover can be the glue to make the final product "pop," they are less manageable and more difficult to perfect. While text is manageable, it can also deviate the eyes and silence the ears if people are straining to focus on the words. Neither is perfect, but they are necessary. There has to be explanatory verbiage to the sights. Which one should the missionary choose? That is a personal decision, but one should ensure the most professional final product. Furthermore, there are other factors to take into consideration. Many churches have blind and/or deaf individuals. Some may not be able to read text, but they can hear a voice; and vice versa. If a missionary opts to have both a voiceover and text, there is opportunity to bless those that are less acknowledged by having inclusive elements within their presentation.

The final concept to ponder is whether or not to add a personal element at the end. This often takes the form of the video displaying the missionary family as they share their heart and/or sending pastor commending them as worthy for support. Again, this is a personal choice, but I would recommend against this inclusion. It adds unnecessary length to the video and can remove the needful intimate connection which takes place immediately following. When a missionary is presenting, the time to share one's heart is personally at the pulpit. As each church has unique qualities and personalities, the missionary can read the crowd to determine the best means of sharing their call and burden. As emotion cannot be equally conveyed nor received via video, it will be hard for a church family to form an intimate bond through it. Also, consider that one's testimony can be lengthened or shortened based on the amount of time available to present if personally performed; a reality that cannot occur if the testimony is on video. Therefore, I believe it is more beneficial to allow the video to simply display the place and the need, while the testimony is utilized to personally and intimately connect with God's people. If one wants to have a testimonial and pastoral recommendation video, create a separate file specifically with that content and a third that has both the presentation and the testimonials. This adds options to fit different scenarios that occur throughout the deputation process.

Overall, the presentation video provides a vital and powerful opportunity to affect the heart of church members unto compassion for lost souls that reside in the uttermost parts of the world. It must have a sense of professionalism and remain current with the personality of the people of the day, but God can and does utilize it for His glory in swaying hearts unto His missional work.

The Testimony of Calling

Hudson Taylor once engaged in a conversation with a long-time missionary to China named Wilhelm Lobscheid. Questioning Mr. Taylor's call to the field of China, the following conversation ensued: "Why, you would never do for China," he exclaimed at length, drawing attention to his fair hair and grey-blue eyes. "They call me 'Red-haired Devil,' and would run from you in terror! You could never get them to listen at all." "And yet," replied Hudson Taylor quietly, "it is God who has called me, and He knows all about the color of my hair and eyes."[17] The power of a testimony is that it finds its source in God. Regardless of the outward features or the judgment of men, when the Lord has divinely appointed a man to mission's work, He will supply for even all that lacks.

When presenting one's testimony before a congregation, it is the time to form a personal connection with the people. It is opening one's heart and sharing on an intimate level how the hand of God manifested itself in the missionary's life unto the strengthening of a church. Before delving into the main content of this section, it is important to address a quick side note. Please always make sure to address the pastor after just being given the platform. Thank him for the invitation and commend his church family publicly on the blessed reception one has received from them. Make it brief, and make it personal and purposeful. Now, forward onto the main content. There are three areas which ought to be displayed in the testimony: A burden for a people, church agreement, and the clear evidence of a calling. [18]

---

17. Taylor, H. (2012). *Hudson Taylor in Early Years: The Growth of a Soul.* Hardpress Publishing.

18. In my dissertation research, I asked a total of twenty-five pastors the following question, "An effective missionary testimony must at least consist of a burden for a people, an agreement in their local church, and a verifiable confirmation of God's calling through Scripture." Of the twenty-five, twenty-one strongly agreed, three agreed, and only one

(1) A burden: Hudson Taylor would often speak on the millions that were swiftly perishing in China; "A million a month, dying without God!" He had a depth of love given to him for the Chinese people that was inexplicable outside of Christ; a burden which moved God's people around the world to action in supporting this work. This has grown increasingly difficult in the modern-day. Many hearts have grown calloused, many churches have grown cold. People are not easily broken for lost souls; especially those in another land. There were times my own family was pressed on the need in our own country for faithful preachers with the added hypothetical slant, "So why go abroad?" Regardless of the reception or the lack of understanding, love the church still. The heartfelt expression a missionary displays for the people they are presenting to and the people they are called to must be clearly evidenced before the congregation. Hate is contagious, but so is love. The former simply spreads more naturally than the latter. One's love will have an impact.

(2) Church Agreement: The local church is the vessel which God sends missionaries through. When a congregation has reckoned the hand of God upon one of their own, it evidences His power for others. It verifies to a pastor that one of his own can be called and it signals to the people that there are proper channels one must pass through to perform certain works in Christ. Mostly every church leader has a strong desire to send a missionary out of his own local body. It is certainly profound to support many from other churches

---

disagreed (with the comment that a personal, verifiable confirmation from Scripture was his only minor point of disagreement.)

going to foreign fields, but it is a spectacular reward in Christ when one from his local body is called and sent. Stand as an encouragement to the pastor that God is still calling from congregations like his to till the ground in unknown lands. If the church leadership feels that fire welling up, one can be sure the people who have their heart will too.

Those that have a calling on their life may then seek the pastor's counsel on the following steps. This is important because there are those that are interested in missions, but seek to "go around" the authority of the local church and the deputation process. The thinking is that they can simply move to a country, use their trade skills to get by, and eventually land in a native church that needs assistance as a staff member. This is not God's design. When the missionary declares that God has called one's local church to stand in agreement and send through His processes, the people will gain a deeper understanding of the operational aspects of sending and going.

(3) Clear Evidence of the Call: A burden is not a calling. I understand this may not be a popular opinion, especially amongst missionaries. I am not trying to sound discouraging or hurtful when writing this. A burden is a wonderful, blessed emotion given by the Lord, but it does not always constitute a calling. Remember, Paul himself *"assayed to go into Bithynia: but the Spirit suffered them not"* Acts 16:7. Yes, he was already a missionary, but the principle stands the same. Though he was burdened for the people of Bithynia, God was not calling him there. Far too often an individual stands before a congregation and confuses his burden with a divine calling. Is it a wonder why certain "missionaries" struggle to receive

127

support while others seem to reap plentiful partnerships? The reason is because there is clear evidence in one and not in the other… and many churches can recognize the difference. While a burden may or may not coincide with a calling, the two are not synonymous (see Jonah).

The evidence of a calling must be clearly displayed before the Pastor and congregation. There is not an occurrence in Scripture where an individual was not chosen by God to missionary service. While a calling "may" take certain forms, the most concrete, verifiable, and direct evidence is founded in Scripture. A passage the Lord has utilized to solidify His will for the individual for which he can then tell the people, "God said to me in His Word 'such and such a verse.'" The Apostle Peter even declared that despite having walked with Christ Himself and having heard the voice of God from the heavens, they had the *"Word of prophecy made more sure; whereunto ye do well that ye take heed, as unto a lamp shining in a dark place, until the day dawn, and the day-star arise in your hearts"* (2 Peter 1:12-21). Rather than simply trusting in personal experiences of life, it was the Scriptures he pointed to as the verifiable evidence of conclusive truth. It is the Word, the still, small Voice, that has the power; not an outward sign that cannot be conclusively founded in Christ (1 Kings 19:9-18).

I recall a time I was waiting for a haircut and I could overhear the conversation between a barber and his client. The conversation was strange as they attempted to tout their own moral superiority to each other and over the rest of the world. During that conversation, the client then spoke about his boxing career. He told a story of a time when he was running for exercise early in the morning as he trained for an upcoming match. During his run, he looked up and saw a shooting star. In his own words, that shooting star was confirmation from the universe that he was walking the right path in life. The barber emphatically agreed. As a Christian, we might raise an eyebrow and purse our lips to the silliness of such a conclusion; and rightly so. Why then do missionaries share similar stories at the pulpit? One reads a country name in a newspaper and declares that place as where God had called him... until it was not. Yes, God can and does utilize signs outside of His Word, but a Christian would be hard-pressed to find any scriptural evidence where God's Word was not clearly spoken or intrinsically involved in accompanying such a sign. Therefore, pastors and church members will be skeptical of those who share their calling as one of flashing lights with the complete absence of the more sure Word.

The testimony is sometimes the only opportunity that a missionary receives to publicly pour one's heart out before a congregation. It is an intimate and brief moment to share, to display, to encourage, to teach, and to challenge a people in mission's work. It is not a time of self glorification, but of strengthening the people. For when the congregation is strengthened, the Lord will greatly move in their heart to open the doors of partnership; even if the missionary has fair hair and grey-blue eyes.

Missionary Sermons

Can missionaries preach? Not whether or not there is

actual opportunity to stand at the pulpit; rather, do they have the ability to preach with power? When it happens, the usual response is, "Wow, he preaches well... for a missionary." It is not difficult to feel the gut-punch in that statement for the current state of missionary preaching ability. If one could only listen to the sermons of the missionaries of old as they preached with the power of the Spirit of the Living God! There are some extant manuscripts, but the Force of the man as the Lord spoke through him is lost in history. How our churches need to feel that power again through missionary voices.

As this book is not a guide on the methodologies of biblical preaching, it will not touch on writing and preparing sermons. The missionary must ensure that they themselves have received the proper training, academically and practically, to deliver well-prepared, Spirit-led material. What will be reviewed are the expectations of missionary sermons. How one can best draw from the word of God to the lighting of a fire in the hearts of His people for missional work.

(1) Prayer and Preparation: There is nothing greater that will connect the missionary to the heart of God's people than powerful preaching. The testimony is needful and mightily used, but a sermon delivered through God's authority is unmatched. This is achieved through prayer and preparation. J. Oswald Sanders stated, "The goal of prayer is the ear of God. Prayer moves others through God's influence on them. It is not our prayer that moves people, but the God

to whom we pray."[19] An abundant prayer life is vital if the missionary is to produce Spirit-moving, missional sermons. Prayer for which passages to preach, prayer to direct the preparation of the sermon, prayer for the reception of the message into the ears and hearts of the listeners, and prayer for the moving conviction of God within them. Proper prayerful preparation for preaching is founded when the missionary has flooded the self, the study, and the people underneath it. I have often heard of pastor's praying not only in their study for wisdom, but at each pew, calling out his members by name unto the Lord, in the early hours of Sunday mornings. A missionary ought to have that same prayerful endurance for the message and the people to whom he is ministering. If one believes that to be impossible, remember how Paul unceasingly prayed for the churches which he had served (Colossians 1:9, 2 Thessalonians 1:11).

A message that has been bathed in prayer is clearly evidenced in one that is not. There is no alternative nor eloquence of speech that can replace the absence of spiritual power in a prayer-less sermon. Therefore, seek the Lord, then seek Him again, and then do not fail to continually seek Him. He has the power to move the people; the power which prayer taps into.

Additionally, a few quick words for both pastors receiving missionaries and those sending them out. For those receiving, let the missionaries preach. Not only is it biblical

---

19. Sanders, J. Oswald. *Spiritual Leadership: Principles of Excellence for Every Believer.* Chicago: Moody Publishers, 2017.

for them to strengthen churches through the Word, but it will also serve to quickly separate the Spirit-filled from those lacking God's power. A missionary may "fake" a good testimony, but they cannot fake preaching with God's power. One does not have to "give up" a Sunday morning service, either. There are Sunday Schools, small groups, age group fellowships, Sunday evenings, mid-week services, and multiple other occasions to preach the Word. Therefore, if a pastor desires to partner with Spirit-led missionaries, let them preach. For those sending missionaries, please do not send them out under-prepared. It is not the duty of a mission board or seminary to take the reins in this vital area. They certainly assist, but the church is responsible for discipleship and development. Struggling on the deputation trail is good, but only if it is necessary in God's design. Unnecessary struggles will only lead to frustrating conclusions for all parties involved, which many pastors have expressed. As sending churches do not appreciate receiving poorly trained missionary speakers, they themselves must endeavor to properly train up their own into knowledgeable, capable speakers.

(2) The Right Focus: It is entirely possible for a missionary to preach a great sermon in the wrong context. Yes, even a mission's-minded message that has the incorrect focus for a specific congregation can cause damage; even when it was purposed to fortify. This is another reason why prayer is vital even after the study is complete. As every church has its own personality with strengths and weaknesses in certain areas in missions during the various seasons of ministry, the missionary must be filled with and

yielded to the Holy Spirit in deciding what topic concerning missions is proper to preach to each congregation.

The fact that there are multiple congregations with varying needs that grant distinct amounts of time to preach necessitates that multiple messages must be prepared. Is it wise to go to war with one bullet in the chamber? Did not David bring five smooth stones to battle against Goliath? I remember a time when I was presenting to a sweet church family on a Wednesday night. I had difficulty reaching the pastor, but fortunately was able to contact him early that Wednesday morning. We went to lunch together when he dropped some harsh words with a heavy heart, "Our church just split on Sunday and I have no idea if anyone will be there tonight." As a young missionary with no experience on church splits, I had no idea what to do, what to say, or what to expect during the services that evening. I took the need to the Lord and asked Him for wisdom. Praise God, I had a certain message prepared that had a missional focus centered around following Christ and keeping our eyes off others. It was exactly what the congregation needed to hear from an outside voice to heal them of their fresh wounds. Following that evening service, the church experienced great revival and growth; a reality that may have not been possible if all that was available was one generic message. Though I never experienced that same circumstance again, I was glad for the prepared Word of the Lord. Every church has to be challenged according to their need and the missionary must be ready to meet that need in Christ.

Therefore, what should a missionary preach on? One word: Missions. Do not stand before a local church and attempt to be an evangelist or their pastor. Do not attempt to batter or beat or bludgeon the people into submission. That is not the missionary's role or purpose. One is there to strengthen the people and challenge them in missions. What about missions should be preached? There are a variety of topics to choose from. One can speak on the "why" of missions, the calling of missions, the giving for missions, the reward in partnering in missions, the result of missions, the focus of missions, etc. One can have a church-wide focus or even challenge the Christians as individuals within the congregation. The truth is the Lord Jesus has a will both for the church body and also the individuals themselves. Maintain the flexibility that preparing several messages allows so that each congregation can be properly stretched and challenged.

Can missionaries preach? This should not even be a question on the mind of pastors or members. Missionaries ought to be fully capable of delivering the Word in the power of the Spirit of the Living God. They ought to be prayed up and fully prepared to engage each congregation with *"Thus saith the Lord."* It is a shame that this question is usually hypothetical; the answer already written on the hearts of the people. There is still time to change the current landscape. Pray and prepare well, that the listeners might hear the Force of the man as the Lord speaks through him.

Time Allotment

"You have five minutes to share your testimony." Five minutes? That is all? It is at this venture the missionary then stands before the congregation and waxes eloquent or, as one of my professors would say, "waxes elephant" for the next ten to twenty minutes. Impossible? No way there can be anyone that blind to time? Think again. This will occur, usually multiple times by different missionaries, at nearly every single mission's conference. A strict time limit is given, but apparently the content is too important to be muddled down to five minutes; therefore, the missionary "waxes elephant" to all in attendance. Trumpeting on and on until soon words become only obnoxious noise to everyone listening, but himself.

Missionaries are notorious for far exceeding the given time limit. Whether the amount of time allotted is five minutes or the entire hour, many have made it a practice to stretch the barriers far beyond their given borders. Please, never do this. Whatever one needs to do to stay within the designated time frame, do it. Have a silent phone alert that shows on the pulpit with ten minutes down to even one minute to the cutoff point. Have one's spouse motion in the congregation with inconspicuous numbered sign cards. Take the necessary time to learn to compact one's testimony to even one minute or less, to speak on only the most essential elements founded therein, and to shorten a message on the fly. Do whatever must be done to ensure that the pulpit has been vacated when the clock strikes quitting time. There are not many occurrences that will sorely rustle the frustrations of a pastor and his church members like a speaker who neglects the time. Furthermore, often other missionaries are to follow whose opportunity will then be cut short and/or the people have already lost attention before their engagement. It is unfair and, quite simply, wrong. There is absolutely nothing that a missionary has to say that is so important it exceeds the specified limits given by the pastor.

With that said, the pastor and people will be extremely appreciative of a time-sensitive missionary. When one can share in the allotted time and, all the more, share powerfully, the Lord truly blesses those moments. Whether or not the individual receives a partnership of support, their name has instantly risen as a reliable entity and will be positively spread amongst preacher friends. Something so simple can have such a profound impact for both good or bad. For oneself, for churches, and for other missionaries, ensure that the impact is positive.

The Missionary's Attire

The battle for proper church attire, especially for those standing in the pulpit, has proponents on both sides of the coin. This section is not purposed to disparage those who hold to another view than what I am about to claim, but I do hope to challenge the missionary on "pulpit attire" by taking the principles of Scripture to display both a biblical and professional perspective. Essentially, how to best represent the Lord Jesus and the calling of a missionary before a local church family.

(1) A Reverent Position: I often think of Joseph when he was summoned out of the dungeon and into the presence of Pharaoh. The Bible records in Genesis 41:14, *"Then Pharaoh sent and called Joseph, and they brought him hastily out of the dungeon: and he shaved himself, and changed his raiment, and came*

in unto Pharaoh." In preparation to stand before the most powerful human ruler on the earth, Joseph needed to make his physical appearance worthy before entering Pharaoh's presence. A similar account is founded during the reign of king David. When David sent his servant ambassadors to Hanun, king of the Ammonites, he incorrectly perceived David's intentions and thus had his servants humiliated with an improper shaving and having their garments immodestly cut. When news reached David, he sent men to meet his servants, who were greatly ashamed of their new presentation, to tell them to tarry at Jericho until their beards were fully grown (2 Samuel 10:1-5). Hanun purposefully attacked the appearance of David's servants, which was a direct insult bearing great irreverence and disrespect to the king's person and position. As the servants themselves were ashamed to stand before their king in their current appearance, David, in considering his position and their predicament, told them to tarry until they were once again worthy to stand before him.

For Joseph, it was only until after the old prison clothes were discarded and the unhygienic appearance made fresh that he was worthy of entering the presence of Pharaoh. For David's servants, it was only until they had the proper clothing and their beards were fully grown that they could return to present themselves and serve their king. Appearing unkempt or even in natural attire when summoned before a ruling presence has historically been frowned upon. Even in the modern-day, one can watch as a championship sport's team meets the President of the United States donning professional attire. Anything less is to appear to show disdain and lack of reverence for the position. If that be the case, how much more so when one stands before the Lord?

The priestly class and especially the High Priest wore specially designed holy outfits as they were serving and appearing before the Lord (Exodus 28). David stripped himself of his own authoritative kingly regalia and wore a linen ephod as he danced before God (2 Samuel 6:14). In the Heavenly Kingdom, believers will be clothed with robes of pure white symbolizing the purity of righteousness founded in Christ Jesus (Revelation 3:4-5, 7:9, 19:7-8). Remember when Moses was met by God at the burning bush? What did God instruct of him to do before anything else? The Lord said, *"Draw not nigh hither: put off thy shoes from off thy feet, for the place whereon thou standest is holy ground."* He had to remove his shoes while standing in God's presence (Joshua was instructed to do the same [Joshua 5:14-15]). This was an Eastern picture of acknowledging one's defilement when standing before the holy God. It was an act of reverence to remove one's shoes, and if one were to forgo this practice it would identify that individual as approaching the Lord with a haughty and irreverent spirit.

Clearly, the type and manner of clothing matters to both man and God. As Christians, our attire is a symbol of both our reverence for the One in the highest position as we stand in His presence, and a defining characteristic for who we are in Christ. Unfortunately, many have lost this understanding. We opt to stand in the pulpit wearing clothing that more closely resembles a sport outing; rather, than a holy meeting with God in the church building. No, the physical building may not be the Temple, but the building is the meeting place that Christians congregate as a local body, as the Temple themselves, to publicly stand before and worship the King of kings. Clearly, the attire of God's people is vitally important as one presents himself and represents the Lord of all.

(2) An Exemplary Position: Christians are representatives of Christ in this world. The Bible declares in 2 Corinthians 5:20, *"We are ambassadors for Christ."* An ambassador is a diplomat sent to a foreign country to serve as its representative. While a worldly ambassador is "on the job," one would never see them wearing anything but professional attire. A polo, jeans, and sneakers are not exemplary when representing a nation.

It is interesting that if one attends an impoverished Haitian church, the entire congregation from the pastor to the children are wearing their very best dress. They comprehend that, even in their poverty, they must represent Christ through their attire in a dark land; their financial and/or physical situation are of no excuse to forgo that responsibility. The Christian's citizenship is in Heaven and, while present on this earth, we directly represent that Holy Land and the King of that Land. As David's servant ambassadors in the example above represented him not only in word, but also in appearance, know that Christians exemplify the Lord Jesus before the great cloud of witnesses in their choice of apparel. Exemplary clothing is needful as it displays one's position and ownership in Christ.

How then should a missionary dress in the pulpit? One must take the principles of reverent and exemplary clothing and infuse it into the cultural expectations of utmost

139

professionalism. No, they did not wear suits in David or Jesus' day, but history has always maintained certain representative garments and hairstyles which displayed both position and respect. Therefore, one ought to appear in what is both culturally professional and reverent before the Lord (God clearly understands and works within cultural expectations of dress, evidenced with Moses and Joshua). While this attire in a country church may slightly differ from one in the city, it is vitally important to adhere to godly and culturally professional etiquette. If one desires to don the garments of their country of calling, first request permission of the pastor and then ensure that it is the exemplary attire of that land. In this manner, both God and the calling are given proper representation and reverence on the holy ground of a local church pulpit.

Extra-Pulpit Communication

What is spoken in the pulpit must match what is displayed in the hallways. How a missionary converses, acts, and reacts will be observed by the pastor and church members. I recall a story of an old evangelist preaching on sin and getting right with God. After the service, a church member approached the man, wanting to shake his hand and thank him for the message. Unfortunately, when the member's hand was extended and tattoos were displayed, the evangelist refused to shake it. How foolish. Everything that was stated in the pulpit was then lost because of one prideful moment of self-righteousness.

Extra-pulpit communication is an intimate extension

of the pulpit ministry where deeper connections are made as the people can shake the hand and share their heart with one they consider a hero of the faith. While missionaries do not consider themselves heroes, it is interesting that we consider those who have faithfully served on foreign fields as our own "heroes." The missionary must remain humble, but also allow people the blessed opportunity to connect with him as he prepares to serve the Lord on their behalf in foreign lands.

The Display Table

The display table is a kind of physical extension of the presentation video. It allows the congregation to touch certain trinkets of the culture, to see the writings of the Bible in foreign tongue, and to further learn of the operations of that people group. As mankind is often naturally intrigued by unknown and uncommon entities, the table will serve as a coaxing mechanism to draw people near and hold their attention without needing to aggressively start and end conversations as the members start toward the exit doors.

There is nothing especially critical to have on a display table. Some missionaries opt to have more items displayed and some less. I would personally suggest having a foreign Bible, a few unique trinkets, and a vertical banner resembling one's prayer card.[20] Ultimately, whatever direction the missionary

---

[20] As a word of caution, if one has a newsletter sign-up, make sure to request permission before placing it on the table. Pastors want to protect their flocks and there have been missionaries that have collected names and then, in future letters, requested finances to help with a need or project. Church members will then bypass the authority of the local church and

decides with their display items, what is important is that one has a "base camp" at the church that the people know where the missionary is typically located before and after service. This helps to maintain the ability to funnel people to one's direction for open lines of communication without much aimless wandering. I would urge, do not find oneself "attached" to the table. Utilize it as a resource, but do not rely on it as the only area of communication. Venture off into the hallways and sanctuary to meet and greet the people. The Lord will surely bless as one reaches out to shake hands of the people.

The Pastor Vs. The People

Teetering on the balancing rope of conversation between the pastor and his church members certainly takes skill, insight, and wisdom. The missionary cannot find himself clinging to the staff of the under-shepherd nor can he completely distance himself to frolic only amongst the sheep. The pastor is the authority that will ultimately decide on the support status of the missionary, but the members play a vital role in urging him to do so. Therefore, the missionary has to quickly assess the attitude of each specific church family and then accordingly attribute their time.

Understand though, one will usually have plenty of opportunity to speak to the pastor. Approach and converse

---

finance them directly. This is a quick way to lose monthly support. My advice is to first request of the pastor permission and then to have at least two separate emailing groups: Pastors only and a total collection. With two separate emailing groups, the missionary will not offend when asking for finances if it is sent directly and only to the leadership of the local church.

with him, but spend significant time with the people. Do not set up in the tower of the king and ignore the townspeople. That is not what he wants. The general desire a pastor has is that the missionary is presentable, approachable, and positively conversational with his people. Often, one will find that leadership will purposefully request the missionary to sit at tables filled with church members during gatherings, drive their people toward the missionary display at the start and close of church services, and even have Q&A sessions to further connect them with the missionary and field. If one can connect to the heart of the congregation, the pastor will connect with the missionary.

Profitable Conversation

A missionary's conversation is evaluated through the strong relationship between their actual words, the tone of their speech, and their body language. The three are individual components that strongly relate to one another. A child who excitedly wants to go to the park will not ignore the huffing and puffing that follows the exasperated "fine" of his parents. Though they all may go, the occasion will not be a joyous one. Profitable conversation demands the missionary prepare for all manner of approach. People, whether leadership or laity, will either knowingly or ignorantly try the spirit of the missionary. Some may ask off-handed questions, tout their clout, or push buttons. Others will bless, encourage, and pray. Learning to converse well demands the filling of the Spirit that the joy of the Lord will infuse itself into one's words and ways for every possible occasion of conversation. As the missionary will experience a plethora of personalities, he must be readied spiritually to handle them with grace.

Before delving into what is profitable, one must understand the opposing type of communication. Unprofitable conversation occurs when there is a negative diversion of at least one of the mouth, the tone, or the body. This diversion will not go unnoticed by observant individuals. Even something as little as constantly peering behind the person directly speaking to them, regardless of one's uppity, positive tone and seeming interest in the conversation, will convey to that individual that there is something more important than the current engagement. While it is necessary to have peripheral knowledge of what is occurring around oneself (especially if the missionary has little children), what is direct is where the focus ought to be. Take note of what occurs in the retail industry. An employee may have their direct attention on a specific customer, but they must also notice others in waiting. The proper etiquette is to quickly acknowledge those in waiting with a glance or short greeting, and then continue to engage the customer at hand. If the conversation is ongoing and lacking needful content, one may attempt to slowly ease toward the other parties. It is a delicate balance so as not to offend anyone, but necessary to ensure one spends the maximum amount of time with as many church members as possible.

Unprofitable conversation also occurs when the missionary is awkward or disinterested in their approach of others. A secluded, disengaged missionary will have difficulty winning the hearts of the people. Winnie the Pooh once said, "You can't stay in your corner of the forest waiting for others to come to you. You have to go to them sometimes."

Go to the people. Some will be naturally shy and unassuming, but they have questions. Approach them and engage them in conversation. Share about the excitement of missions and of one's prayer requests, ask them about their church and thank them for their heart. Whether brief or drawn-out, people will appreciate a missionary that is desirous to break bread at "their table."

One final aspect of unprofitable conversation is when the missionary delves in the realms of subjects such as politics or touchy doctrinal issues. Even the soundest churches will have members and visitors with strong conclusions in each playing field. The first piece of advice would be to avoid and divert these conversations at all costs. They are not profitable and, even if one agrees with the person, there are listening ears nearby that may not. If total avoidance and diversion is not possible, make sure to have biblical, generic responses spoken in joy that magnify Christ and place the emphasis on Him and the pastor. Phrases that can be modified to various situations can be, "Yes, we are praying and trusting in the Lord to bring His will to fruition" and "I appreciate you asking, but I think that would be a better question for your pastor to handle." The missionary is not at the church to fall into a trap of disagreement, argumentation, or to "right" erroneous beliefs of certain members. One is there to be an uplifting, strengthening presence; therefore, avoid and detract from touchy subjects while seeking to quickly revert back to what is good.

Profitable conversation is called profitable because it holds value. There is a long-lasting advantage that branches from it. It demands an acute knowledge of oneself in any present moment, of the personality of the immediate congregation, and of a specific individual at hand. The missionary has to present themselves in all aspects with fullness of joy and passion for the work without leaving any legitimate opportunity for a person or the church body to form negative conclusions. Be wary and on guard, the devil will utilize any means to disrupt at least one component of the missionary's communication. Receive the fullness of the Spirit beforehand and seek His continual filling, including during one's public ministry. He alone will uphold and maintain the man.

(1) Build Connections: People connect through shared stories and similar experiences. Members will most certainly speak to the missionary about their field and how they themselves had experienced that culture in certain ways. The opportunity to build connections in a short time occurs during these brief moments. The missionary must take advantage to engage in that conversation by listening to their stories, sharing one's own, encouraging and thanking the individual for their heart, and asking them about their personal life (nothing too personal, of course). One will be amazed at how people will open up and talk about their children and grandchildren, military past, travel experiences, and the like. This builds a strong relationship between the missionary and the church members that leads to receiving intimate, continual prayer. A person will remember to pray for someone who impacted their life, regardless of how fleeting the moment.

(2) Pray for Needs: As wonderful as it is to hear the blessed stories of church members, one must remember that

they also have prayer requests. Pains, hurts, and challenging situations abound that must be laid before the throne of grace. The church in Corinth were reckoned by Paul as faithful in partaking together with him in his sufferings through prayer (2 Corinthians 1:7-11), but Paul himself also prayed continually for the churches he served and their members (Colossians 1:9, 2 Thessalonians 1:11). It is not simply the duty of the church members to pray for their missionaries, but also for the missionaries to pray for the churches. I recall a church member telling me of a dire situation forthcoming for which I told her I would pray. Her reply was, "Don't worry about that, you are too busy to pray for me." Break that thinking! Ask for prayer requests and, if able, pray for them immediately in their presence. Deliver their needs before the Lord Jesus Who is able to hear and answer. Display great love for the people by rejoicing and praising God in their victories and bearing sympathy and encouragement through Christ in their trials. A missionary that openly prayers for the people will likewise receive mighty prayers in return.

Profitable conversation holds eternal value. Christ utilizes it for His purposes in the lives of many who are impacted by those who show an interest in them. How often stories are told of the "giants of the faith" extending out a hand to "regular people," moments which the Lord used to change the entire trajectory of those individual's lives for His glory. Rather than huff and puff and blow the house down, build the strength of the people and the church.

The Bible details how powerful the missionaries were when presenting in local churches. They were vessels of strengthening in Christ through the delivery of His Word.

Partnerships were made and the message of hope plunged forth unto the reaping of souls and the discipling of believers. The expectations for modern-day missionary communication are not unfounded. These same expectations required back then are what are anticipated today. Pastors want to invite those who are capable, professional, and, most importantly, biblical speakers to charge them with God's Word. As the missionary applies the prescriptions and principles founded in Scripture and couples them with the contemporary audience, the Lord, the churches, and the self will be satisfied.

Summary Remarks

Missionary communication will either bring forth fruit unto harvest or tear the roots and defile the soil. A green thumb missionary has honed the art of effective communication by exalting the Lord and strengthening a church family through His Word unto lasting, convicting action. As that harvest comes forth in the form of prayer and financial support, the missionary will soon conquer the mountain of deputation and set their sights on the many majestic peaks of the country of calling.

Chapter 5
Balancing Time

Time is a precious commodity, but often it is seemingly fleeting for the workman. The sun appears to rise and fall as if it is merely changing positions under the cold sheet of the horizon. Redeem the time? Many missionaries are merely trying to keep pace without losing their breath! Suddenly, Rip Van Winkle and his twenty-year, overnight slumber does not seem so preposterous.

The demands of the home alongside the deputation ministry are often overwhelming, ever-increasing, and time consuming. The unfortunate side effects of an unbalanced schedule, much to Satan's pleasure, is the forsaking of the work and, often times, the destruction of the family. Far too often an unbalanced, disorganized, and improperly prioritized daily agenda is the downfall of the workman. As the Lord is the God of order, He expects His children to maintain a state of orderliness in prioritizing their life.

Time Redemption

The desire of the Lord is for the Christian to make the opportune choices in accordance with the shortness of time. The book of James makes it clear that life is as a vapor, like the steam that rises from a pot, it is seen and then swiftly disappears. Therefore, opportune choices are those founded and centered in the will of God. Ephesians 5:16 defines this living as redeeming the time. The word "redeeming" has an interesting root denoting a purchase. It is fascinating to think that the Lord wants His children to "buy" the time; to take ownership of it. The time of one's own lifespan is not to be flippantly discarded or relegated to another user. We have to take claim of it and then utilize it wisely; refusing to allow the evil days to distract the individual from the will of God.

Simply because a missionary has surrendered to the call does not mean that they are effectively redeeming the time. Time redemption is a continual choice, a repeatable purchase. It demands that even the moments of the day are redeemed. How does one spend spare minutes? Or hours? Archibald MacLeish wrote a poem describing the life of a man as an idiotic circus. Strange, crude events occur with no certain meaning until one day the black curtain is drawn symbolizing an eternity of nothingness. Similarly, Samuel Beckett in his play, *Waiting for Gadot,* has two men conversing for the entire duration of the drama as they wait for this gentleman, Gadot, to arrive. He never does. This is his typification for life. People are just killing time, waiting for nothing. Of course, the Christian would vehemently disagree with the conclusions of these two men. We know that this life is precious and eternity is filled with the glories of those who have placed their faith in Him. The unfortunate reality is that, though we might disagree with these men, often times we live life just as they describe. We juggle time around and wait for God to arrive. "Where is He? I surely would have thought He would have shown by now! Maybe I will do this... or maybe that? How about here or how about there?" And one day the curtain of this life closes… and we stand before His very presence; never having fulfilled the fulness of His will.

Our God cares for the birds of the air and the flowers of the field. He even had a prophetic will for a donkey years before it ever walked the earth (Matthew 21:1-5). Assuredly, He has formed the missionary, He knows him, and He has had a will for his life before he was ever conceived. The question is, does he know it and is he redeeming the time to fulfill it? Ephesians 5:16 is surrounded by calls to walk circumspectly, to be wise, and to maintain the filling of the Spirit. These do not occur once and forever remain. They are states of being that demand a heart filled with His Word and a supreme focus on Christ. The following sections will speak on the general structure of time redeeming activity for every Christian, and then the final section will touch on the personal applications for a deputation missionary.

The Great Pendulum

In the 17th century, Christiaan Huygens, a Dutch mathematician, physicist, astronomer, and inventor, developed the pendulum clock. He manufactured his clocks and even had multiple within his own home. During one specific night when he was feeling ill and resting in bed, he noticed a certain, strange phenomenon about them. Though he was sure that his clocks had not commenced their swinging in complete synchronization, he watched as every pendulum swayed in perfect unison. He arose from his bed and restarted every clock, purposely resetting them to break the uniform rhythm; yet, in about thirty minutes, they soon

151

were aligned once again. It was later that scientists discovered the cause of this phenomenon. It is stated that the clock with the largest rhythm has certain sound pulses which travel and pull the others into synchronization with its own.

Imagine a room of pendulum clocks all swinging with a different momentum and constantly ticking at varying intervals. Each clock, without any defined lead, demanding its voice be heard over the others by drawing attention unto itself. It would be chaotic and, quite frankly, immensely irritating. Chaos is never an environment of positive accomplishment and security. There has to be a unifying presence which draws in the surrounding elements to bring a peace to the disorder. Such is the need of the missionary's busy schedule. All matters are not and cannot lay on equal footing. There must be the greatest, the greater, and the lesser priorities; lest the individual find himself in a chaotic mess. Therefore, one must define the unifying presence. This must be the Lord Jesus. He is the Great Pendulum of the Christian life. He is the only "Force" capable of pulling all matters into perfect synchronization within Himself. It cannot be God and... God and the wife and children, or God and the schedule and the travel, or God and schooling and sermon preparation. These matters have a place, but they do not trump Christ nor find equal footing at the top. The Lord alone stands at the pinnacle of priority. Time with Him is of absolute necessity.

I believe that the unfortunate reality for the call to strengthen our relationship with Christ through prayer and the reading of His Word has developed into an almost rattling cliche in the mind, rather than a most necessary rallying cry for the saints. This has partially developed because of the elevation in society and churches of verifiable, quantifiable, visual results. Missionaries, pastors, churches, and Christians all want to see progress and to realize it in a timely manner. As personal Bible reading and prayer are not measurable, they are often set to the backburner as other "more pressing" matters find prevalence. Prayer letters to supporting churches are not filled with one's daily Bible reading habits and prayer journal entries, but with results and prayer requests for results. Therefore, we set keen focus on tending the plants with the expectation of an absolute production of fruit; as if that fruit was formed by our own hands. "Why did such and such occur? Because I did this and that." Then we praise God for the increase. It is a wonder that glory is often attributed by man to God, but I wonder if He is able to receive such glory when He, the only One Who can actually produce the fruit, is rarely sought or called upon. Is He able to be glorified when little time is afforded unto Him in seeking His direction, His Word, His provision, His handiwork? Was the Lord glorified when David and his men took back the Ark, but forsook the Word of God in its transportation? They danced as if He was; at least until Uzzah was struck down by the mighty hand of the displeased God. I am not intending judgment. The busyness and outward expectations of life are assuredly real, but I would beg the Christian not to mistake the graciousness of God in providing fruit as His approving of placing a task, albeit a righteous one, above Him. We can dance and praise and shout His Name, but if that ark is being carried by one's own strength and methodologies; what glory has the Lord really received?

Take a look at Joshua 7. This is a fairly well-known

chapter of Scripture where the children of Israel were overtaking the Promised Land and had prepared to wage war against a relatively unassuming city called Ai. Joshua, energized by the previous victory, had sent a smaller portion of warriors to overcome them. Much to his shock, the Israelites were turned back, thirty-six men died, and the hearts of the people grew discouraged. What had occurred? They were promised of God that no foe could overtake them! The Lord's answer? *"Israel hath sinned."* A certain individual had transgressed the Word of God causing iniquity to be in the midst of the camp. The Lord then ended His speaking by stating, *"Up, sanctify the people, and say, Sanctify yourselves against to morrow: for thus saith the LORD God of Israel, There is an accursed thing in the midst of thee, O Israel: thou canst not stand before thine enemies, until ye take away the accursed thing from among you."* The unfortunate reality is that Joshua had failed to reckon the Lord for the current situation. Though He sought the Lord in past circumstances and was promised victory over the inhabitants of the land, he assumed that God was with him against Ai... until he realized, far too late, that He was not. Though God had not removed His promise of victory, there was sin in the camp that caused a fissure between them and the Lord: *Thou canst not stand before thine enemies, until ye take away the accursed thing from among you.* If they were to receive power from on high, the situation would have to be dealt with accordingly. The people were ordered of the Lord to sanctify themselves by heeding His Word and then ridding the sin from their camp. If Joshua had only sought God before sending troops to overcome Ai, there would have been no loss of life nor lessened morale.

While Christ is immeasurably longsuffering, His patience does run dry. He will not allow His child to continue on devoid of His presence. When sin is in the camp and/or self is at the forefront, cities like Ai, or rather the fiery darts of Satan, will cause destruction. The missionary must always be sanctified and centered in the Lord. One cannot bypass seeking and drawing near unto Him simply because of successful prior campaigns. He is the needed strength. He is the gracious provider. When the pendulums of life swing, He is the unifying beat. Chaos is not found in those who are daily centered in the Lord, but in those who have exhausted every avenue of human capability only to realize that we are powerless to make the fruit grow. Mankind is created to love and worship the Lord. He is the Great Pendulum of life and the Force of unity for what would otherwise exist as absolute disorder. As Christ Jesus Himself stated, *"But seek ye first the kingdom of God, and his righteousness; and all these things shall be added unto you."* Seek Him first; He will ensure that all these things, the blessed fruit, shall be added unto the man.

Peanut Butter and Jelly

Navigating through the various elements of work and home are a challenge that every family must face as both maintain demands that require the allocation of self, time, and resources. With the difficulties often multiplied in ministry, how does the missionary balance them?

While there is no perfect example, I want to open this topic with an illustration of food. Every culture has a unique food pairing. Japan has raw fish and rice, the United States has peanut butter and jelly, and so on. I will stick with PB&J for this illustration. The formation of a peanut butter and jelly sandwich is quite simple. It takes the two elements of peanut butter and jelly and then combines them on slices of bread. This works because the independent elements are a cohesive pair. They are not at odds; rather, they work together. The sandwich maker also has opportunity to choose which element has more of an emphasis; more jelly than peanut butter and vice versa. However it is made, one also realizes that even though they can pair together they are still independent of each other. There is still much remaining in the jars of peanut butter and jelly that have not yet combined. These can be utilized for another sandwich or even remain completely independent as they are utilized for another purpose. This is much like the relationship between the family and the ministry.

The family is a major component, but so is the work. The missionary's duty is to reckon that the two elements are both important, understand that they are also independent, and learn to balance the two as a complementary, cohesive pairing when necessary. The family is a ministry, but it is not the ministry. The ministry will affect the family, but it is not the family. The two are independent, but they also intertwine often. It is common to witness the following mistakes when attempting to balance them: One element is often highly elevated over the other (all ministry and no family; vice versa), the two elements are completely and forever combined without independence (ministry cannot be done without the family and family cannot exist without the ministry), the two never combine (a total separation of the ministry and the family), or both are disregarded and lost because of inadequate management.

Properly balancing the ministry and family is akin to peanut butter and jelly. They are independent elements, but they have the ability to seamlessly and cohesively pair together. Though there will be times when the Lord requires the missionary to make tough choices, they are not involved in a competition of superiority. Sometimes a decision must be made to spread more peanut butter (family) than jelly (ministry,) but if one has already relegated the proper balance between the two, the other will not feel forsaken and forgotten.

I think we have had enough PB&J, what does the Word itself declare? 2 Corinthians 7:32-35 directly references the attitude of the single and married. If one is single, full attention can be afforded unto the Lord without the cares of the home. There lies the opportunity to maintain consistent attention to the work and service in Christ. If one is married, the cares of the world are necessary. This is not referencing worldliness; rather, the goodly aspects of marriage in caring for a spouse and child(ren). The Lord designates the care of the family upon those that have, which inevitably demands time split with the ministry work. Furthermore, husbands and wives are to love each other as they fulfill the certain God-ordained positions within the home (Ephesians 5:22-33.) Those in pastoral ministry have a command to care for the home as proof of their ability to tend to the local church (1 Timothy 3:4-5.) The very fact that the qualifications of a pastor require that they are already properly stewarding their own home before entering ministry displays that the family stands on the higher prioritized ground, but again the two are not opposed nor in competition. They are independent, but they work together; and there are times sacrifices will be made on both ends.

Essentially, the missionary's priorities after Christ are his family and ministry, with a slightly higher elevation for the family. After the Lord, the majority of one's remaining time for the day has to be fitted into serving these two elements. What good is the ministry if the family has been lost? What kind of shepherd allows the family to destroy the ministry? Learn to balance the elements individually, but also focus on how each pair together when the many opportunities arise. The Lord God will give grace in both.

The Ministry of Rest

Personal time is vital for the health and longevity of the missionary. It is never intended as a vacation away from the work of the Spirit in the life of the believer. The missionary cannot simply put off the armor for a day in the sun. I will admit that respite is often relegated to the lowest rung of the ladder, but it is still a rung; nonetheless. The ministry of rest is purposed to result in a spiritual and physical revitalization.

The book of Genesis declares that God Himself rested on the seventh day; a pattern for which He commanded of the Jewish people on the Sabbath (Exodus 20:8-11). Part of the purpose of this was to foreshadow the rest in Christ to come. He is our rest. Outside of Him, there exists no peace nor repose for wearied souls. Jesus Himself offered His ultimate rest to any and all who would come to Him (Matthew 11:28).

It is in this that the missionary must continually find himself. It is the rest void of worry, anxiety, cares, and sorrow. It is rest from the fleshly attempts to please God or to somehow earn His approval by works. Christ's yoke is easy and His burden is light… He is the rest for the weary.

Another purpose of the Sabbath was for the Jewish people to have a weekly repose for the body and mind. God cares for one's physical well-being. Regardless of the spiritual strength of the missionary, a machine, no matter how well-built, will eventually malfunction if it is not properly cared for. An unhealthy body and/or overwhelmed mind will severely incapacitate one's ability to consistently serve with proper form and function and will eventually cause a rift between the man and his priorities. Rest, health management, and pleasurable activity is like oil in the joints. As indicated in 1 Timothy 4:8, physical health and bodily maintenance have profit. They may have a lesser worth than the spiritual, but they have profit. Paul encouraged Timothy to care for his health (1 Timothy 5:3,) the believer is encouraged to maintain a mentally strong mindset in Christ (Romans 12:2, Philippians 4:8,) and the Bible is wrought with God's instructions and promises for bodily maintenance. Jesus Himself took opportunities to rest with His disciples (Mark 6:31; Luke 8:23; Matthew 14:22-23). Caring for the body and mind may have lesser value than the eternal spiritual foci, but God's man will struggle to serve well if there is the lack of physical maintenance.

Let us take an example from the life of Elijah in 1 Kings 19. He was one of the holiest prophets to minister upon this earth, but even he suffered breakdown. As he was fleeing for his life from Jezebel, he fell into a state of severe depression and anxiety wishing himself to die, *"He requested for himself that he might die; and said, It is enough; now, O LORD, take away my life; for I am not better than my fathers."* It was at this moment that the Lord powerfully and wonderfully displayed His love unto His servant. He firstly sent an angel to renew his physical body with nourishment that he might bear the journey ahead. Twice did this occur as Elijah was requiring proper rest and restoration to his body. The next matter to handle was his mental state. After his body was rejuvenated, he left for the cave and mountain wherein he would hear the Word of God. Upon arrival, he poured his heart out unto the Lord saying, *"I have been very jealous for the LORD God of hosts: because the children of Israel have forsaken thy covenant, thrown down thine altars, and slain thy prophets with the sword; and I, even I only, am left; and they seek my life, to take it away."* His thoughts and mental state were in flux. Essentially, he believed himself to be the only one faithful in the land and even then his life was threatened by the hand of the ruling authorities. God replied, *"Go, return on thy way to the wilderness of Damascus: and when thou comest, anoint Hazael to be king over Syria: And Jehu the son of Nimshi shalt thou anoint to be king over Israel: and Elisha the son of Shaphat of Abelmeholah shalt thou anoint to be prophet in thy room. And it shall come to pass, that him that escapeth the sword of Hazael shall Jehu slay: and him that escapeth from the sword of Jehu shall Elisha slay. Yet I have left me seven thousand in Israel, all the knees which have not bowed unto Baal, and every mouth which hath not kissed him."* He was telling Elijah not to fear nor be dismayed. He had His hand upon the ruling authorities and, as a means of encouragement, informed him of the seven thousand who have remained faithful in the midst of evil. God set to restore Elijah's physical well-being that he might return to the ministry refreshed and renewed.

As a missionary, rest is a vital piece of the formula for consistency and longevity in the ministry. It is not always available on a daily basis, but it is essential to schedule and perform. The difficulty lies in "escaping" the busyness. "How can I focus on myself? It seems impossible to have alone time to rejuvenate." I would encourage the missionary to look to Christ Who ensured Himself and His disciples a time of self-nourishment away from the crowds. This time has to be scheduled, or it will not be accomplished. My pastor had always implored me to schedule rest; otherwise, I would never find it. Scheduled respite can take many forms. It can be as simple as a daily walk, involvement in sporting events, or a solo trip to the store. It is not always the exercise that is performed, as much as it is the time alone to provide small refreshers to help alleviate stress and mental blockage. Vacations, spiritual retreats, and other forms of elongated periods of relaxation are also needful for one's long-term spiritual and physical well-being. Deputation often covers *at least* ten total months each year of constant travel. I would urge the individual to schedule a restful retreat for one or two weeks as it will do wonders in easing the burden, revitalizing the spirit and body, and fulfilling the call.

Applying the Priorities in Deputation

The road does not always afford a set schedule. People often appreciate their day spread out neatly, but deputation often has a mind of its own. How then can one make time for the Lord, the family, the ministry, and rest? This is a difficult question to answer because of the unique element that is every missionary (Single vs. married, children, travel distance, other priorities, etc.), but there are principles which one can employ to ensure a full measure of fulfilling one's priorities.

(1) Make the Time: Whether at home or on the road, excuses can abound. While on deputation, there is also the extra added factors of road fatigue and schedule exhaustion. The missionary must never excuse one's way into failing to uphold the ministries of life. Whether one chooses to wake up early, fall asleep late, or switch around certain daily programs, there are always creative ways to make the time count.

(2) Ridding of the Lessers: It was Winnie the Pooh who said, "Sometimes the smallest things can take up the most room in your heart." We tend to compartmentalize our life and withhold certain things from the hand of Christ. Certain sanctuaries in our heart which we need to rid ourselves of that tug away at our daily minutes and hours. They tend to be trivial, but they serve as idols by remaining at the forefront of our mind and far too often distract and deviate from what is necessary and essential. The missionary needs to either keep these under submission (if it is neutral in Christ) or rid themselves of it altogether (especially if sinful). A trivial thing is of no worth to destroy the home and ministry.

(3) Plan with Purpose: A deputation schedule may have loops and twirls with plenty of uncertainties, but that does not mean one cannot plan. Each day assuredly brings times of stillness that can be filled with spiritual development, family outings, or romantic dinners. While the weekly "Friday Night Pizza and Movie" may not always be possible, one can still plan

with a purpose. What days consist of short drives or are even absent of the road? What are the conference schedules like? Are there stores nearby to visit or city walks to stroll along? My wife and I would often plan ahead activities so that we had events to look forward to that broke up the humdrum of the schedule. She also planned crafts for our little one. We had ice cream nights and strolls together. It was not always easy, but it was possible. Plan with a purpose!

Summary Remarks

Our time is precious and to abuse or misuse it is an affront against the Lord. We are not to juggle it around seemingly willy-nilly with no plan or preparedness. The Lord has expectations for us in redeeming the time; making the best use of the life He has given us for His great Name. The missionary schedule is no exception. It is not enough to merely fulfill the base elements of travel. It is not sufficient to drive, stop, and present in an endless rinse and repeat cycle. Fill the days with Christ, the family, and His work... and schedule rest when it is needful. Order the moments. He will surely bless!

Chapter 6

Prepping for the Move

John Thomas, a fellow missionary with William Carey, scribbled the following to his friends in London just before their departure, "13 June - The ship is here - the signal made - the guns are fired - and we are going with a fine fair wind. Farewell, my dear brothers and sisters. Farewell. May the God of Jacob be ours and yours, by sea and land, for time and eternity! Most affectionately adieu!"[21] With the climax of deputation, the sights of the missionary are set on embarking with a fine, fair wind toward the land of calling. The mountain is nearly conquered and the preparations are now underway to a new home and ministry. There is assuredly a concoction of emotions vying for position in the missionary's heart. One's thoughts are probably centered on spending time with loved ones and the imaginations of life in a distant country. Yet, with the final countdown underway, one cannot lose sight that there are concluding items on the agenda to tackle before "boarding the ship and sailing away."

Prepping for the move to a foreign land has certain aspects that are both specific to each individual missionary and general for all. As there are such a wide range of

---

21. Drewery, Mary. *William Carey: A Biography*. Grand Rapids, MI: Zondervan Publishing House, 1984.

specificities, I cannot possibly cover all of them. For example, each country has their own set of rules and regulations regarding visas, entrance requirements, ministry legalities, etc. Furthermore, missionaries have backgrounds from all walks of life and must prepare the move in a manner which suits their own self and family in Christ. Will one sell his possessions or store them? Will the family sell or rent the house? What is to be shipped over? Intricacies that are country and missionary specific must be handled according to one's own context.

However, there are principles for which all missionaries can glean from as one prepares for life and ministry in a foreign field. This chapter determines to highlight these areas as a means to prepare the missionary for the move leading to a less stressful transition. [22]

Financial Considerations of Deputation

A mountain nearly conquered is not conquered yet. Do not make the mistake of jumping off a cliff edge that stands thirty feet above the ground because one "might" survive the fall. Why hamper oneself? Yes, the missionary may survive such a foolhardy decision, but then having to continue on with "broken bones" (or worse) is certainly unwise. Whatever gains one made with that "leap of lack of faith," they will be

---

[22] It is important to note that, at the time of writing, I was finishing my own deputation. The following are principles that I have learned through either first or second-hand knowledge. Though everything listed was not personally experienced, this does not discredit the second-hand knowledge gleaned through others.

lost while attempting to inch forward with the injuries of unfinished business.

The Lord has called the missionary to fulfill the ministry, not to abandon it in the final stages. Could we imagine Paul skipping over his divine purposes of strengthening churches and fulfilling his calling on the home front? Of course not. Neither should the missionary make excuses to justify pre-mature departure. The last moments of an arduous endeavor are often the most challenging to fulfill, including those on deputation. As the country of calling is within sight, one's bags might be packed and plane tickets purchased, but there is still work to be accomplished. Leaving without completing that work will cause one to have to push through greater and unwarranted adversities; in addition to what the world and the devil are already sending. The final descent is needful and necessary for easing the short-term transitions and for providing long-term sustainability.

Reaching 100% Support

When is it finally time to draw the line on church presentations and turn one's full attention to arranging the home and preparing to board the plane? While this question certainly has nuances per the individual, there are some factors one must take into account: current support level, projected support level, and long-term support level.

The financial aspect of missions is a key component to living and performing ministry. There are missionaries that arrived on the field fully supported and others that were short on finances (some far short), who then consistently struggled to the detriment of themselves and others. While the root of the issue in leaving for the field before full support is raised is an overzealous spirit and a lack of faith in God's full provision, missionaries will often make the claims that the need was too great to wait and the support amount was simply an exaggerated number. There are even those that claim that living under-supported takes "real faith." This is simply a prideful excuse coated in religiosity. Is it "real faith" when the missionary had, in lack of faith, sidestepped God's design and thus are then suffering needlessly? Is it really a testimony of God's goodness when the missionary and family are struggling to make payments to even afford the basic cares for themselves and the ministry? I love how Daniel 2:21 writes, *"He giveth wisdom unto the wise, and knowledge to them that know understanding."* This means He will give more wisdom and more knowledge to them who are living in His current given wisdom. Essentially, if one is living faithfully in the wisdom of God for their life right now, He will then assuredly direct their next steps. As that is the case and promise, one can then surmise that the contrary is also true. If an individual is not faithful, then God will not give more wisdom and knowledge until they are.

Skirting God's design is not real faith, but it is an exhibition of a lack of faithfulness to the current wisdom given by the Lord. The unfortunate reality which is soon realized by the under-supported missionary is that there is a limit to frugality in living and ministry expenses. The individual will soon find his family suffering and thus asking for money from fellow laborers on the field, churches and individual Christians back in the States, and, if desperate enough, the nationals themselves. That "real faith" is actually a real burden to anyone connected with the individual.

Full support is like a vital organ formed by God to pump feasibility into the missionary's living and ministry. When that organ is strong and operational, there is the total financial capability to accomplish necessary tasks. If that organ is unhealthy or withering away, the entire body of the missionary's life and work will be in a state of financial arrest. Can the Lord jumpstart that member with an infusion of finances? Of course! But why should He have to? He had set a definitive mark at the commencement of deputation for the overall support number and it was the missionary's responsibility to faithfully endure that ministry until the Lord brought the financial goal to fruition. Is He then liable to continually provide where one has fallen short in faith and faithfulness? He is not... but His mercy and grace far exceed our own. Therefore, if a missionary is under-supported, I would urge that individual to praise God for His generosity, thank Him for His mercy, give glory to Him in His provision, but to not test His patience. Return to the States and finish raising support.

When does the missionary stop booking churches and start focusing on the transition? One must evaluate the three levels of support noted above to form a conclusive answer. The current support level is derived from calculating only the total actual monthly finances received. It is not a combination of the actual and promised amounts. The promised is certainly a welcome infusion when it arrives, but many promises have fallen short over the years. Know what is definite, and pray for, but do not rely on, the promised. The projected support level is when a departure date has been set based on one's current support level, the peace of God, and the number of church presentations that are still forthcoming. By now, the missionary has a stronger inclination of which churches are more likely to support a visiting missionary and which ones are up in the air. This projected support level is really a prayer request made in the faith and peace of God that He has determined such and such a date for departure and, with that date, He will also bring in the final fruits of the harvest as one finishes the final presentation schedule. Finally, the long-term support level is a projection of ongoing support determinable immediately upon stepping foot on the field. This is a long-term view based on what one believes will most likely last for a lifetime subtracted by what has the potential to be lost. While I do not have the studies and statistical analysis, I have been told that some missionaries have lost upwards of 20% of their overall support upon initially reaching the field. That is a monstrous amount! It is not hard to imagine the stress one might feel if that occurred after departing under-supported. Any missionary would cringe at such a loss.

After evaluating these three levels of support, the missionary is to then make a decision. How many churches are needed to reach that full amount before departure? Would it be better to raise upwards of 110% to offshoot any potential losses in the immediate or coming future? With these questions in mind, one must have the peace of God, the prayers laid before His throne, and the wisdom to act in accordance with His given wisdom. It is impossible to determine the number of churches needed in this book for the reader because every missionary's current and needed support level is different. Therefore, the individual must take these general principles and infuse them into one's own context to determine the proper answer. If I can urge anything, trust the Lord and reach 100% support, if not more. The line can finally be drawn once one has finally passed that threshold.

Raising for Savings

Every missionary must take into account the astronomical costs of moving to a new country and the multiple ministry expenses in the near and distant future. Tens of thousands of dollars are spent, nearly immediately, on visa documentation, shipping goods, securing and furnishing a new home, paying for language school, vehicular transportation, and other early large cost endeavors. Future plans, such as for a church plant and building projects, demand even more finances. The only way to possibly pay for these expenses is to prepare for them.

Raising and saving commands the missionary has a firm grip on managing personal finances and has actively submitted requests to partnering churches. The work cannot be accomplished if the missionary is incapable of properly stewarding God's money and/or if the partnering churches are stingy and unwilling to supply. Rarely is the latter the issue. I would urge any individual, if they do not have a needful depth of understanding of money management to undergo financial training before leaving for the field. With that said, one must have a plan of preparation to secure these monies.

(1) A Reserve Account: A reserve (savings) account is a priority for every missionary. The substantial funds raised for future costs must be sent to a secured deposit that the individual does not readily withdraw from. This will allow a continual infusion of monies over the course of deputation that is solely purposed for future heavy costs. Though fundraising will be spoken of shortly, the missionary must remain cognizant on setting aside certain funds into this account. By evaluating one's own monthly budget sheet, a fixed amount can be strategically placed into savings from monthly support. Greater infusions will find their source from love offerings and fundraising.

(2) Love Offerings: There is a certain balance every missionary has to make when it comes to booking meetings. "Regular" meetings consist of any given weekly service that has no special event connected with it, while missions conferences are solely focused on missions, missionaries, and financial support. There are certain advantages and disadvantages that come with each. With regular meetings, a missionary can attend upwards of twelve to fifteen churches in one month (a lofty goal), but mission's conferences often are prolonged events that can severely condense one's scheduled meetings per month. While regular meetings are more often a "shot in the dark" as far as support and love offerings are concerned, mission conferences have a much greater chance of receiving monthly support and often supply higher love offerings. With regular meetings, the missionary has the chance to arrive on the field sooner given the larger number of possible opportunities, with conferences the missionary may take a longer approach to have a more secure

chance of support per visit. While the goal of visiting a church is not simply financial nor to "speed through" the deputation process, raising money and reaching the field in a timely manner are still important factors.

From a purely financial perspective, conferences are well intended, though not guaranteed, for one to gain support and obtain substantial love offerings. Missionaries have received offerings ranging from $500 to even exceeding $10,000 from a single conference. These are critical to not only assist the missionary in their travel and living expenses, but to save for the future. When receiving substantial offerings, whether it be a regular meeting or a conference, the missionary must have the mindset to save a certain amount. If this is properly performed, one's funds will continue to accumulate and, when nearing the end of deputation, several thousands of dollars can be saved and set aside to pay for large expenses.

(3) Fundraising: Requesting finances for a specific need is an endeavor that a missionary personally organizes from supporting churches. This should never be performed over social media or any format outside of the local church. Do not seek out individual church members to be one's "donors." The biblical model is for the members to send finances through their local church which then is collected and sent to the missionary (Philippians 4:10-23; 1 Corinthians 16:1-3; 2 Corinthians 8:1-7). With that said, there is the proper channel to perform fundraising.

The pastor of the church maintains the authority as the under-shepherd of God to collect and send finances to any missionary. It should be he alone (or a subsequent staff member in charge of missions) who is contacted for financial needs. This request can be made in-person, over the phone, or through a personal prayer letter. An in-person request is generally made after the pastor himself has approached the missionary about one's financial needs. This opportunity, if it comes, will usually take place when presenting within the church. This demands the missionary be readied with an answer. A phone call is rather self-explanatory. The missionary will personally communicate with the pastors of one's supporting churches and lay out the need and answer any of their questions. A personal prayer letter is also a viable and popular option. These fundraising letters should never be sent directly to church members. One should have an organized set of email addresses where they are directly and only delivered to the pastor, his secretary, or the staff member leading the mission's ministry. To avoid any confusion or misunderstandings, it may even be beneficial to add a short disclaimer which states that the letter had not been disseminated to personal members. As a general outline of communication for fundraising, the missionary ought to establish the need, why meeting it is the Lord's will, and how the churches can help to financially cover the expense. When the fundraising goal has been realized, a formal "thank you" should be immediately sent detailing the Lord's provision, thankfulness for the heart of the churches that prayed and provided, and that no more funding is needed. In this manner, the missionary has glorified the Lord, intimately involved the churches in His work, and proved oneself as a reliable, trustworthy vessel with finances.

Raising for saving is actualized when the individual

has the foresight to prepare for the coming unavoidable, substantial expenses. If these are not planned for or the missionary is not proactive in raising and saving, the individual will immediately be hampered before even leaving for the field. Commencing on-field ministry in debt is a poor testimony of financial stewardship and a red flag for partnering churches. Therefore, receive financial counseling, have a full knowledge of forthcoming expenses, and be motivated to ensure that one is readied to properly and effectively cover the needs of the field. In this manner, God is glorified and the work is accomplished.

A leap is not of faith if it is performed outside of the will and direction of God. It is a leap of impatience, a leap of overzealousness, a leap of disregard… a leap of lack of faith. Raising financial support and savings takes time, dedication, and planning, but the Lord will bless the faithful efforts of the missionary. If one has not yet properly conquered the mountain, the bags ought not yet be on the ship as there is a work yet to be accomplished. Churches need strengthening, support needs raised, and lessons need learned. Remain faithful in the descent, the end is drawing nigh.

Preparing for a New Life

In preparation for the Doolittle Raids of WWII, it was said, "As the mission was quickly approaching, the men, instead of playing cards, began to pour over maps of Japan. Now there was much less idle conversation and no laughter could be heard. When it came time for the men to turn in, many went to sleep with their clothes on."[23] Transitioning to on-field ministry is not a lifelong vacation, but a war for the souls of man. It is the laying of one's life down for the purposes of God. Deputation is the "combat training" for the front lines of spiritual and physical battle. Now, as the man readies for the mission, the missionary must rise and sleep equipped with the armor of God. Always at the ready for when the Commander issues the charge to go and do battle amongst the spiritual forces of evil.

Living in America is drastically different compared to living in a foreign land. Even predominantly English-speaking nations have vast distinctions in living, cultural intricacies, etiquette, speech patterns, cuisine, religious beliefs, etc. There will assuredly be spiritual and physical attacks as the enemy of souls seeks to destroy the man of God. If the missionary is to properly prepare for this battle, there are spiritual and physical aspects of transition to take note.

The Spiritual Transition

Moving from the United States to the field of calling is somewhat of a transition from light into darkness (though this is becoming increasingly less accurate). At home, there is a foundation of Christ within one's circle of fellowship and church family. When transitioning from a land with a long-tenured history of Christianity to one that has been lost in the clutches of darkness for hundreds, if not thousands, of years,

---

23. Goldstein, Donald M., and Carol Aiko Deshazer Dixon. Return of the Raider. Lake Mary, FL: Creation House, 2010.

the missionary may be taken aback by the spiritual heaviness that surrounds him. While a survey trip may have given a glimpse into the absence of Light, there is nothing outside of the Spirit of the Living God that can adequately prepare one for residing within it. C.T. Studd's famous quote eloquently describes this drastic change, "Some want to live within the sound of church or chapel bell; I want to run a rescue shop within a yard of hell." It can be cozy next to the church, but running a rescue shop in the midst of "hell" is to set a light on a hill where everything is engulfed in darkness… a darkness which especially desires to even consume the man of God.

The spiritual transition onto the field demands a close proximity to Christ and an endeavoring to continually draw ever nearer; despite what is to come. He is the One residing within us. He is the Buckler and the Strong Tower. He is the Ever Nigh. To leave His fortifications necessitates that one is wandering in the darkness. That happened to the Apostle Peter. He was powerfully serving the Lord, until his three-time denial wherein he fell into bitter sorrow. Following the aftermath, the Bible declares in John 21 that he fell back into his old trade of fishing. He was essentially "wandering in the darkness," no longer as near to the Lord or serving Him. Yet Christ in His goodness pulled him off of those old boats and back into service. He was going to again live for God and, ultimately, perish as a martyr for His glory. When Jesus finished speaking to him, He gave a very important charge, "Follow thou Me."

John Benton once stated, "The coal which falls out of the fire very quickly goes cold." While Peter was working those fishing holes, the cold darkness was the reigning victor extinguishing his brilliant light. He could not bring glory to God while residing outside of His fortifications. It was only until he returned to His presence and service, by the mercy of the Lord, that the light of Christ would burn brilliantly again through his life and death. Missionary, remain near to God, but know that even if one is wandering in the darkness the Lord desires to pull one off those boats and back into Christ-glorifying service. Where He goes, go. What He directs, do. When He restrains, withhold. Follow thou Him. He has called one to serve in the darkest trenches amongst the very gates of hell. Draw near to Him. Draw ever nearer to Him. Then run the rescue shop, shine the Light, and bring God glory.

The Physical Transition

The transition of the body and mind to a foreign land with different customs, behavioral patterns, living conditions, speech and linguistics, and the like will require a serious change of mindset and acclimation if the missionary is to make an impact for Christ. There will be many facets of society that are strange and, in our Western eyes, awkward. For example, in Japan there is the culture of bowing; as opposed to shaking hands. It is much more intricate in design and is strictly followed within the society. Depending on one's age, rank, and relationship (and other factors), one will receive a deeper bow signifying greater honor. While this is natural to the Japanese people, a Westerner may initially struggle with understanding the etiquette involved and when to properly execute a well-timed, rightly angled bow. It might be awkward and uncomfortable to greet people in such a manner, but to do so is at the heart of the culture.

That example is merely one small drop in a bucket containing the many vast intricacies within societies. Preparing the physical body and mind to distort itself into uncomfortable situations that are neutral regarding the law of Christ will take time, wisdom, and preparation. The individual has to gird oneself with the mindset of Paul; willing to give up his own Christian liberties to honor the Jews, the Gentiles, and the weak in all manners and customs that are neutral to the Law of Christ (1 Corinthians 9:19-23). A false understanding of Christian liberty is one of the greatest hindrances to the advancement of the Gospel and the sanctification of souls. A false understanding declares, "I am; therefore, I will." A biblical understanding declares, "They are; therefore, I won't." When entering the field, do not flaunt one's liberties as an excuse to refuse to partake in neutral customs. Dive in, enjoy them, and honor the people. Show them that it is fully possible to live as a good Christian and as a good "Asian/African/Mediterranean/etc." The Lord will utilize it to open the doors of their hearts for His glory.

Readying for the First Matters

Before plunging forth headlong to the ministries of the field, there are certain matters to attend. There will be visa applications and governmental paperwork to fill out, housing accommodations to secure, language training to apply for, schooling for the children, and other such important matters. The difficulty in writing on these elements is that all of them are unique per the missionary and their situation. What is able to be handled is the generic understanding that there is work to be accomplished and, if it is not, there will not be a ministry (at least not for very long).

As the missionary prepares to leave, he must have advisors that can assist in guiding him in these subjects. A mission board, a missionary, a national, one's sending church, and government officials can and should be inquired of to properly and swiftly progress forward. The more well-organized and efficient the missionary is, the less opportunity for errors and delays. Make sure to receive all of the necessary information that one may make wise decisions so as not to hinder the family or the ministry. The devil will certainly weave his web of aggravation. Unknown hiccups and seemingly unbelievable problems will arise, but the Lord is good to handle these situations. Pray and prepare well, everything will work together according to the Lord's will.

Tempering Expectations

It is nearly impossible to strip oneself of expectations in various aspects of life. I remember an individual once openly state that he holds the lowest expectations possible when venturing into new experiences, that way he is pleasantly surprised when he has a good encounter. I cannot say I necessarily agree with his stance, but it makes the point that those who hold elevated expectations are frequently met with disappointment. If we were to take a moment for introspection, we would often find that we fail to meet even our own measured goals and expectations for our own life; how much more so will outward experiences come short in our eyes? Therefore, as one prepares for the coming transition, there has to be a cognitive understanding that there will be pleasing experiences and difficult hardships that are contrary to what was fully anticipated. One must have a measured and sustainable balance for what is to come.

With many great transitions of life, there is often a honeymoon phase at the outset. When the missionary arrives on the shores of a foreign land, the food and language and cultural oddities are all thrilling and interesting to the constant captivation of one's attention. This has been the long-awaited desire and the individual ought to soak it up. Venture out, explore, and make mistakes. Talk to the people and form relationships; the Lord will use the missionary even in the early parts. These experiences will help the transition feel smoother as one absorbs information about one's new home and surroundings. Unfortunately, it does not take long for the honeymoon stage to end. Studies determine that this phase commences into culture shock following the second to third month. Culture shock arrives with the frustrations in the language barrier, the maneuvering through foreign obstacles and issues, and the surplus of general discomforts. Bills have to be paid… in a foreign language. Groceries have to be purchased… in a foreign language. Doctor visits have to be made… in a foreign language. Laws, customs, signs, gestures are all different. The food, though tasty, is missing the comforting flavors of home. Yes, culture shock is real and the frustrations will mount if one is not prepared for them beforehand. Overall, the general consensus is that it takes the average person about one year to grow fully accustomed to this new transition of life, though I am sure the timetables vary depending on the individual.

Assuredly, the Lord has been steadily girding the

missionary for tempering one's expectations of a foreign land through what has already occurred via deputation. Certain church expectations have either come far short or greatly exceeded what one initially anticipated pre-arrival. Certain pastors and church members may or may not have been as open and welcoming. Though early on this may have been rather frustrating, the Lord continued to prove Himself good and the missionary then learned to temper his expectations and trust in the Lord. One must ensure that this transitions to the field. Yes, it is invigorating and long-awaited, but there is a reason why many missionaries remain in service but only a few short years on the field before returning home. On a practical level, learn to balance optimism with reality while trusting all things in His hands. As He has called, He will also strengthen the man through coming frustrations.

The new life will demand the exorcizing of certain aspects of the old. The way in which Westerners view daily physical and spiritual matters will assuredly change when ministering in a foreign nation. This does not mean to forgo the Word or ministering in a manner that glorifies Christ, but to rearrange oneself to live and maneuver within a new culture that is firstly glorifying to God and secondly honorable to the people.

Summary Remarks

With the mountain nearly conquered, the ship in one's heart has certainly readied itself to sail away. The land and the people are no longer blocked by the mountain, but are simply a step beyond the horizon. As the missionary endeavors to finish the final stretch of the deputation ministry, the glory is all due the Lord. He has shown Himself faithful, able, and glorious. He has utilized, provided, and prepared the man. As the final descent is underway, take a moment to praise Him. He is the reason one has endured, He is the reason one is going, and He is the reason many will come to know Him as Savior in that land. Therefore, take a moment to reflect and thank Him... and then humbly request that He would now move before into the hearts of the people as He sends his servant to deliver His Word.

Conclusion

I would urge the reader, never allow sight to hinder one's faith. The spiritual always exceeds the material; the invisible to the visible. The mountain of deputation is not an unconquerable entity. Many have gone before and claimed God's Name on the other side. Many have given testimony to the faithfulness and provision of the Lord as they defeated that mighty stone in His power. And furthermore, though the process was trying, many are able to look back in retrospection and thank Christ Jesus for how He used the missionary and prepared him for the sake of others.

I pray that this work was an encouragement to the reader. My desire in writing it was to break down the barriers of surrender and encourage the children of God to faithfully heed His calling. The world needs Christ. People need to hear the Good News. A missionary once wrote,

> This morning I looked at the bleeding feet of a missionary, saw his wife tending them, saw the blood and pus running from them and thought to myself, "What a nauseating sight that is!" But, as I walked from the room, the Lord kept saying to me, "Oh, but to Me they are beautiful feet!" Then I remembered—"How beautiful upon the mountains are the feet of him that brings the good tidings"—good tiding to men and women like those in New Guinea who sit in darkness and in the shadow of death. Someday it will all be over. Someday the tired, bleeding feet of the missionaries will for the last time cross those broken-bottle limestone mountains. Someday for the last time they will go down into one of those newly discovered valleys. Someday for the last time they will speak the message of redemption through Jesus

Christ our Lord. Someday that last one will turn to Jesus. Then the clouds will part asunder and our Savior will be there.[24]

Very soon, Christ is returning... but as for right now there are millions of lost souls who God has called His children to reach with His Word of salvation. As Paul penned in Romans 13:12, *"The night is far spent, the day is at hand: let us therefore cast off the works of darkness, and let us put on the armour of light."* May it never be said that deputation was a hinderance to His will for one's life. May it never be said that souls were lost to the eternity of hell because of a measly slab of stone. Rather, when Christ returns, let Him find us in the fields.

---

24. Rose, Darlene Deibler. *Evidence Not Seen.* Harper & Row (HarperCollins), 1991.

About the Author

Nick Zarrella was approved as a missionary to the nation of Japan in May of 2019. He served as the Children's Pastor at Plantation Baptist Church in Plantation, Fl. During his deputation ministry, the Lord placed a burden within his heart for assisting missionaries in the work and calling of Christ. He has earned his Master of Divinity from Pensacola Christian College and is nearing the completion of his Doctorate of Ministry. He has been married to Lorena for 3 years and has two young children, Levi and Luca.

www.ingramcontent.com/pod-product-compliance
Lightning Source LLC
Chambersburg PA
CBHW071437090426
42737CB00011B/1691